TARTANS
THEIR ART AND HISTORY

'Nowhere beats the heart so kindly
As beneath the tartan plaid'
                                    Aytoun

ANN SUTTON & RICHARD CARR
TARTANS
THEIR ART AND HISTORY
PHOTOGRAPHY BY DAVID CRIPPS

ARCO PUBLISHING INC
NEW YORK

NOTES FOR AMERICAN READERS

1. The words 'tartan' and 'plaid' tend to get confused in their journey across the Atlantic:
   Tartan is used to describe the checked fabric which is the subject of this book.
   Plaid should be reserved to describe the simple primitive garment originally made by sewing together two 27-inch widths of handwoven tartan cloth, each 12 feet long, making a piece of about 5 feet × 12 feet to be used as a garment or blanket. The word does not, in Scotland, refer to the tartan patterning.

2. Weavers will probably realize that the British term 'shaft' is the American 'harness'.

NOTES FOR WEAVERS

Because the technique of weaving tartan cloth is basically the same as in weaving any other fine grade of twill fabric, details of 'how to thread the loom' etc. are thought to be unnecessary and all 4-shaft looms suitable for cloth weaving can, of course, be used for weaving tartan. Most weavers would agree, however, that for anything larger than a scarf, a floor loom is preferable to a table loom. To the best of my knowledge there are no specific yarns available to the handweaver for the weaving of tartan cloth; it is a matter of selecting good quality yarns in the colours required from the usual suppliers. Care must be taken to select the fibre, yarn and sett (used in the sense of the number of threads per inch) which will produce a cloth suitable for the purpose envisaged — a soft woollen spun yarn, or silk, with a loose sett for a scarf, for example, and a worsted yarn, closely sett, for any fabric which is to resemble that of the traditional kilt.

Ann Sutton
1984

ACKNOWLEDGEMENTS

The authors would like to thank the following for their assistance in the preparation of this book:

Malcolm R. Innes of Edingight CVO WS, Lord Lyon King of Arms
Dr D Gordon Teall of Teallach, Chairman and Vice President, The Scottish Tartans Society
Dr Micheil MacDonald FSA (Scot), Director, The Scottish Tartans Society
Peter A. Eslea MacDonald FSA (Scot), The Scottish Tartans Society
W. G. F. Boag MA, The Scottish United Services Museum
James D. Boyd OBE DA FMA
Captain J. Stuart Davidson FSA (Scot)

Thanks are also extended to:

The staff of Arundel library for their unflagging and cheerful assistance
Gil Mohan, for research help
Elizabeth Henson, of the Rare Breeds Survival Centre
Kenneth Dalgleish, of D. C. Dalgleish Ltd, Selkirk, for supplying all the tartan samples illustrated
Wendy Haberl, for her cheerful assistance in the preparation and checking of endless thread counts and details
The Scotch House of Knightsbridge for the 'List of Family Names and their Clan Tartans' and for their general interest
Methuen & Co. Ltd, London, for the extract from *In Scotland Again* by H. V. Morton
The Natural Dye Company for the loan of the yarns photographed on page 40/41

The authors and publishers also wish to thank the following for permission to reproduce photographs:

Bodleian Library, Oxford, page 11; Bridgeman Art Library, pages 1 'Twa Bairns' by Sir John Everett Millais, and 160; British Museum, London, pages 24 (photo John Freeman) and 167 (photo Octopus Books Ltd.); Camera Press, pages 161 below and 162 (photos Patrick Lichfield) Canongate Tolbooth Museum, Edinburgh, page 20 (photo Octopus Books Ltd.); Mary Evans Picture Library, page 34 right; Benjamin Fraser, page 25 (photo Mike Davidson); Glasgow Art Gallery and Museum, pages 8 and 164; Imperial War Museum, London, page 175; International Wool Secretariat, page 36; Mrs. A.M. MacDonald, page 43; National Galleries of Scotland, page 5 'A Highland Wedding at Blair Atholl' by David Allan; National Library of Scotland, page 12; National Portrait Gallery, London, page 159; National Trust for Scotland, page 51; Ann Ronan Picture Library, page 34 left; Routledge and Kegan Paul, pages 38 and 39; Scotsman Publications Ltd., page 179; Scottish Library, Edinburgh City Libraries, page 181; Scottish National Portrait Gallery, pages 27 and 165; University of Reading, page 35.

Photographs on pages 17, 19, 21, 28, 29 and 166 are reproduced by gracious permission of Her Majesty Queen Elizabeth II. Copyright reserved.

Textile photographs are by David Cripps.

This edition distributed by
Lark Books
A division of Lark Communications Corp.
50 College Street
Ashville, North Carolina 28801

Published 1984 by Arco Publishing Inc.
215 Park Avenue South, New York, NY 10003

Copyright © 1984 by Ann Sutton and Richard Carr

All rights reserved. No part of this publication may be reproduced, stored in a retrieval system or transmitted, in any form or by any means, electronic, mechanical, photocopying, recording or otherwise without the prior permission of the publisher.

Designed and produced by
BELLEW PUBLISHING COMPANY LTD.
7 Southampton Place, London WC1A 2DR

Library of Congress Cataloging in Publication Data

Sutton, Ann,
    Tartans: Their Art and History

    Bibliography: P.
    Includes Index.
    1. Tartans   II. Carr, Richard.   II. Cripps, David. III. Title
DA889.H76586 1984   746.1'4   84-6488
ISBN 0-947792-007

ISBN 0-668-06189-8

Printed in Great Britain

CONTENTS

Acknowledgements 4

Introduction 8

The history of tartans 10

The weave 30

Sett and scale 32

The yarn and spinning 34

Dyes and dyeing 40

Handweaving a tartan cloth today 46

The design of a tartan 48

The tartans 52

Tartans of the royal family 158

Regimental tartans 164

District tartans 172

Foreign tartans 174

Lord lyon king of arms 178

List of the main highland clans and map 180

The scottish tartans society 182

Highland games and list of addresses 184

Alphabetical list of family names and associated tartans 185

Bibliography 190

Index 191

Detail from 'Alma: Forward the 42nd' by R. Gibb.

INTRODUCTION

Tartans are inextricably associated with Scotland, even though they are also found as far afield as India and Australasia, Malaya and the Americas – everywhere, in fact, that has connections with the 50 million people of Scottish descent who are scattered across the face of the earth. But tartans are more than a symbol of Scotsmen or Scottish ancestry: they are woven into the fabric of Scotland's history, a living reminder of the ancient clan system that was effectively destroyed by the defeat of the Scottish Jacobites in 1746. They are a symbol of both the ancient Royal House of Stewart and the close links with Scotland upheld by the Royal Houses of Hanover and Windsor; and a reminder that, under all these Royal Houses, Scottish regiments have fought for the defence of Britain at home and the control of an Empire overseas.

Less tangible but perhaps even more fascinating are the myths surrounding the origin of tartans, their development as a means of clan identity, and the belief in an ancient lineage that surrounds so many tartans today. The tartan is the only textile ever to be banned from use (on pain of death). Tartans were brought back to life, first by Act of Parliament; second, through encouragement by Court fashion; third by documents purporting to be of ancient origin; and fourth, by a demand for tartans that led to the Scottish Highlands being scoured for designs that could be put into production by the trade. And in all this, those who actually wove the tartans played a crucial part.

So, besides describing the roles played by kings and queens, heralds, chiefs and military commanders, this book looks closely at the detailed structure of the tartans, the way their design has been influenced by both locality and the weavers themselves, and how methods of spinning, dyeing and weaving the wool have changed over the centuries.

Tartans are as alive today as they have ever been and new tartans are constantly being created. The efforts that are being made to register both Scottish and Canadian tartans in the Court of the Lord Lyon in Edinburgh, and to record all known tartans by the Scottish Tartans Society in Comrie, Perthshire, are described in this book, as are the histories and function of these distinguished bodies.

As General Sir Colin Campbell said to his Highland soldiers as they stormed a rebel fort in India in 1857,

'BRING FORRIT THE TARTAN!'

THE HISTORY OF TARTANS

> It is the best dress fitted for the country of the Gael: intersected as it is by rivers and streams from their native hills, and exposed to the severity of a northern climate, they required a dress which united the recommendation of lightness and comfort, and *in no other dress are these so completely obtained* as in that which as a plaid, formed during the day a graceful ornament, and at night a comfortable covering when forced from their pastoral employments to repose upon their native heath . . . It is an ancient dress, a martial dress, and a becoming dress . . .
> – Sir Walter Scott.

Everyone associates tartans with the Highlands of Scotland, yet to the true Highlander, the speaker of Gaelic, the word 'tartan' does not exist. In fact, it derives from the French *tartaine,* which originally referred to a particular French kind of cloth, regardless of its colour. The true Gaelic word is *breacan,* which is derived from *breac,* meaning 'chequered' or 'variegated'. Chequered garments are known by names such as 'breach', 'brecan', 'brycan' and 'breacan' and appear to have been common not only among Highlanders, but also among the Irish, the ancient Britons and Celtic tribes throughout Europe. There is even a reference to them in Virgil's *Aeneid* – *'Virgatis incent sagalis'* or 'Their cloaks are striped and shining' – though there was no Latin word for tartan as such and striped in this context meant stripes crossing each other from two directions, that is, checked.

As well as being associated with the Highlands – a geographical area north of an imaginary line running from Loch Lomond in the west to the Moray Firth in the east – tartans are also associated with the Highland clans, and in particular with specific clans. Thus today, if you are a member of a clan or of a related (and dependent) family, known as a sept, you can wear the clan tartan. You may also wear the tartan of your sept, if this is different: in fact, there is no law preventing anyone wearing a tartan, though a few tartans are reserved for royal use only. Despite all the publicity given to clan tartans, the truth of the matter is that most of them were invented in the 18th and 19th centuries, and that very few tartans today go back to before the Jacobite uprising of 1745. And then, most of them belonged to *regions* rather than to specific families. Furthermore, in the beginning they probably signified rank and status: it is said that servants wore clothes of only one colour; rent-paying farmers clothes of two colours; that officers wore three colours and chieftains five; while the druids or poets wore six and the Chief or King, known as *Ard-righ,* wore seven. Whatever the truth of this – and there is no written evidence of this before possibly fanciful descriptions written in the Middle Ages – what is certain is that the history of the tartan is steeped in myths and romantic associations, and marked by bloodshed and cruelty. And in these respects, there is no other cloth to equal it.

The beginning of the Highland dress – and thus the tartan – goes back to Scotland's links with Ireland, and the Gaelic tribe which emigrated from Ireland and established the kingdom of Dalriada in Argyllshire and the islands of the Inner Hebrides in the 7th century AD. These early Scots wore the *leine croich,* a shirt dyed with saffron or another bright colour, and a mantle known as a *brat* – a dress which seems unlike any other worn in Europe at the time, apart from the *peplos* and *chiton* worn in Greece. Like other north European tribes, they also wore tight-fitting 'trews' which were like footed leggings that encased the legs separately and reached down to the ankles. This was a garment that probably came from the Gauls in France, since when the Romans conquered Gaul they called the territory *Gallia Braccata,* which means 'the land of the behosed Gauls'. Trews were certainly worn in Ireland by the 10th century AD and were known in Gaelic as *triubhas* or *truis.* There is a reference to them in the 9th-century *Book of Kells.*

For the first 200 years following their arrival in Scotland, the Irish/Scots did little more than engage in constant wars and alliances with the neighbouring Picts and ancient Britons, and the beginning of the Scottish kingdom dates from AD 843, when King Kenneth MacAlpine conquered Pictland and established his rule over most of Scotland north of the Firth of Forth. The main areas outside his control were Shetland, the Orkneys and the Western Isles, which were still ruled by the Vikings.

During this period of Scottish history, the earliest reference to Highland dress probably occurs in the *Saga of Magnus Barefoot,* written in AD 1093, which tells of the Norwegian King returning from a visit to the Hebridean Islands of Scotland and adopting the costume

ILLUSTRATIONS FROM THE *Recuil de la diversité des habits* OF 1562, SHOWING, LEFT HIGHLAND WOMAN IN A SHEEPSKIN MANTLE AND, RIGHT, HIGHLANDER IN AN IRISH GARB.

of that area. Thus he went about barelegged, having short kyrtles (tunics) and upper garments which may well have left his buttocks completely naked. In another description of Scots travelling through France en route for war in The Holy Land, Guibert of Nogent wrote in his *De Vita Sua* between 1104-1112:

> You might see the Scots, fierce in their own country, unwarlike elsewhere, barelegged with their shaggy cloaks, a scrip hanging 'ex humeris', coming from their marshy homeland.

Two points to notice here are the reference to the bare legs and to the 'scrip'. This word derives from the Greek *sytarchia* meaning a container for a soldier's provisions. It was probably an early form of sporran.

Other early references to Highland dress relate to the Church, and it must be remembered that the early Church, with its outposts on islands like Iona and great centres of learning in places like St Andrews, was extremely important in Scotland. There are references to tartans, for example, in the cartularies of the Episcopal See of Aberdeen, where the statutes of the Scottish Church of 1242 and 1249, and the ordinances of the See of Aberdeen of 1256, direct that all ecclesiastics be suitably dressed by avoiding red and green striped clothing, and by not wearing garments that were shorter than the middle of the leg. MacGregor describes the external clothing of priests in the early Scottish Church as

> a wide, loose, flowing garment called the Robe of Offering, a square or oval cloth having in the centre a hole through which the head was passed. It was usually striped or chequered with eight colours, to indicate that while officiating the priest was superior to the King who, according to our ancient Court etiquette, wore seven colours in his tartan, while others wore fewer according to their rank.

ILLUSTRATIONS FROM JOHN SPEED'S MAP: 'THE KINGDOM OF SCOTLAND OF 1662'

Probably the first *visual* evidence of Highland dress, however, relates to the military, and there are figures of Highland warriors among the hoard of chessmen in walrus ivory found at Uig on the Hebridean Isle of Lewis which dates from circa AD 1200. Two centuries later, stone effigies in, for example, the Inner Hebridean island of Islay and in Gluisk, Co. Galway, in Ireland show soldiers wearing what appears to be a pleated kilt, though in fact it was a long, padded, sleeved coat with vertical quilting called an 'acton'. The soldiers were probably Scottish mercenaries known as 'gallowglasses', and their dress cannot have been much different from that of the Highlander described by John Major in his *History of Greater Britain* published in 1521:

> From the middle of the thigh to the foot they have no covering for the leg, clothing themselves with a mantle instead of an upper garment, and a shirt dyed with saffron. In time of war, they cover their whole body with a shirt of mail of iron rings, and fight in that. The common people of the Highland Scots walk into battle having their body clothed with a linen garment manifoldly sewed and painted or daubed with pitch, with a covering of deerskin.

The 16th century, in fact, is notable for both its descriptions and its illustrations of Highland dress. We know what was ordered for King James V to make a court costume of Highland dress when he toured the Highlands in 1538 (an ell measured just over 37 inches):

> $2\frac{1}{2}$ ells of 'varient collorit velvit to be ane Schort Heland coit' at £6 the ell
> $3\frac{1}{4}$ ells of 'green taffatus to line the said coit with' at 10/- the ell
> 3 ells of 'Heland tertane to be hoiss' at 4/4d the ell
> 15 ells of 'Holland claith to be syde Heland Sarkis'.

One cannot be sure whether the short jacket of variously coloured velvets lined in green taffetas is 'Heland' because of its short style or because it was tartan. The 'hoiss' presumably meant trews, but whether they were in Scottish tartan or a type of cloth imported from France is also not certain. The King also asked for Holland cloth to make his long shirts and ribbons for his wrists. The accounts do not mention plaid, bonnet or accoutrements, presumably because these were already in existence, and when all were put together, they must have made the King look every inch an *Ard-righ*.

With King James decked out like a tartan peacock, there is evidence that by the 16th century, special tartans were being worn by some clan chiefs and their immediate relatives, often in the form of silk plaids. A softer tartan cloth, the *breacan*, was worn as a dress tartan by the womenfolk, while a thicker, coarser cloth, *cath-dath* (from *cath*, 'war', and *dath* 'colour') was worn by men, both at work and at war. There was also a special sett for the clergy, the *Breacan nan Cleireach,* in plain blue, black and white, though the use of chequered silk tartans during celebration of the Eucharist was banned by the Reformed Church (circa 1560), as was the wearing of tartans or plaids by Ministers or Readers during a service. Instead, the Church stipulated that 'their habite be of grave colour, black, russet, sad gray, sad brown or searges . . .'. Gaiety in dress was no less anathema to John Knox and his followers than gaiety in any other aspect of life. And attempts were even made to ban women from wearing a plaid. In the 1580s, for example, Aberdeen women were banned from wearing it out-of-doors: if they did, they were considered loose and up to no good.

It was also a time when wearing the tartan distinguished the Highlander from the Lowlander in Scotland. As Nicolay d'Arferille noted in 1547:

> Those who inhabit Scotland to the south of the Grampian mountains are tolerably civilised and orderly and speak the English language; but those who inhabit the north are more rude, homely and unruly, and for this reason are called Wild. They wear like the Irish the large and full shirt, coloured with saffron, and over this a garment hanging to the knee, of coarse wool, after the fashion of a Cassock. They go bare headed and let their hair flow very long, and wear neither hose nor shoes, except some who have boots made in an old fashioned way, which come as high as the knees.

And George Buchanan, writing in his *Rerum Scoticarium Historia* of 1582, describes how the Highlanders use their clothing as camouflage, wearing what are obviously tartans, though there is no suggestion that they are *clan* tartans:

> They delight in variegated garments, especially stripes, and their favourite colours are purple and blue. Their ancestors wore plaids of many colours, and numbers still retain this custom, but the majority now in their dress prefer a dark brown, imitating the leaves of the heather, that when lying on the heath in the day, they may not be discovered by the appearance of their clothes; in these rather than covered, they brave the severest storms in the open air, and sometimes lay themselves down to sleep even in the midst of snow.

What these two descriptions do not make clear is the difference between the Highland commoner and those of higher rank, who wore both bonnet and hose and did not go about bare headed and bare foot. However, the connection between the Highlander and the Irish was noted by the Scottish Lowlander, who called both 'Redshanks' because of their bare legs and knees.

Just what the Highlander looked like can be seen from several contemporary illustrations. *The Recuil de la diversité des habits* published in Paris in 1562 shows a Highlander wearing an Irish-looking garb, with a mantle of herring-bone pattern decorated by fringes, and calf-high boots with variegated cuts around the top, while a Highland woman wears an enormous furry sheepskin mantle. More obviously Scottish is the man shown in a manuscript written and illustrated by Lucas de Heere circa AD 1577. He is bare headed and wears a long-sleeved checked tunic with a pleated skirt, has a mantle over his right shoulder and flat brogues on his feet. And he is armed with a claymore and a long dirk.

The distinction between the Irish and the Scots became clearer when warriors from the Western Isles went to Ireland in 1594 to join the fight against the English Queen, Elizabeth I. Then the Scottish soldiers could be recognized by their mottled, fringed cloaks, and their belts worn outside their cloaks, and over their loins. The cloaks were the origins of the plaid – or, in Gaelic, *plaide*, which means blanket – and became known as the *feileadh-mor* or 'big wrap' or 'covering', which in turn became the *feileadh-beag*, or little kilt, shortened to *philabeg* or *filibeg*. The plaid was worn by laying a belt on the ground and placing the plaid over the belt, folding it lengthwise into a series of pleats. The wearer then laid down on top of the plaid so that he was parallel to the pleats and folded the material on either side of him over the front of his body, fastening the belt around his waist – a forerunner to the modern kilt – and a mass of material above it. This would sometimes be allowed to hang down at the back or it could be arranged over the shoulder or – in bad weather – form a protective covering around the neck and head.

The different ways in which the plaid could be worn are shown in Van der Gucht's military drawings of the 1740s. It could also be used as a blanket roll when sleeping out rough on the hills, and for bedding in less uncomfortable circumstances. And, because it usually measured 5 × 14 or 16ft, the width was beyond the reach of a hand-thrown shuttle and so two widths of 19-25 inches were sewn together. An exceptionally detailed description of the plaid was given by Martin Martin, who was factor to MacLeod of MacLeod, in his *Description of the Western Isles of Scotland* in 1703:

> The Plad wore only by men, is made of fine Wool, the Thread as fine as can be made of that kind; it consists of divers Colours, and there is a great deal of ingenuity required in sorting the Colours, so as to be agreeable to the nicest Fancy. For this reason the Women are at great pains, first to given an exact Pattern of the Plad upon a piece of wood, having the number of every thread of the stripe upon it. The length of it is commonly even double Ells; the one end hangs by the middle over the left Arm, the other going round the Body, hangs by the end over the Left Arm also. The right hand above is to be at liberty to do anything upon occasion. Every Isle differs from each other in their Fancy of making Plads, as to the Stripes in Breadth and Colours. This Humour is a different thro the main Land of the Highlands in-so-far that they who have seen those Places is able, at the first view of a Man's Plad, to guess the Place of his Residence.

Martin's description gives a clear indication of the strong influence the weavers themselves probably had over the colours and designs of the various tartans.

If the plaid marks the beginning of what is now regarded as traditional Scottish dress, its use with tartan hose and a blue bonnet was established by 1618 when John Taylor travelled from London to Braemar to join a hunt organized by the Earl of Mar which was attended by nobility and gentry. Taylor writes:

> . . . where they do conform themselves to the habite of the High-land men . . . their habite is shoes but with one sole apiece; stockings (which they call short hose) made of a warmer stuffe of divers colours, which they call tartane; as for breeches, many of them, nor their forefathers, never wore any, but a jerkin of the same stuff that their hose is of, their garters being bands or wreathes of hay or straw with a plaid about their shoulders, which is a mantle of divers colours much finer and lighter stuff than their hose, with blue flat caps on their heads, a handkerchiefe knit with two knots about their necke; and thus they are attyred . . . As for their attire, any man of what degree soever that comes among them, must not disdaine to wear it; for if he doe, they will disdaine to hunt, or willingly bring their dogges; but if men be kind with them, and be in their habite, then they are conquered with kindness and sport will be plentifull.

There is also another delightful description of the Scottish Highlander by William Sacheverell, Governor of the Isle of Man, who visited the Hebrides in 1689. He says:

> During my stay I generally observed the men to be large-bodied, stout, subtle, active, patient of cold and hunger. There appeared in all their

actions a certain generous air of freedom and contempt for those trifles, luxuries and ambition which we so servilely creep after. They bound their appetites by their necesssities, and their happiness consists, not in having much, but in coveting little. The women seem to have the same sentiments, though their habits were mean and they had not our sort of breeding, yet in many of them there was a natural beauty and a graceful modesty, which never fails of attracting. The usual habit of both sexes is the plaid; the woman's much finer, the colours more lively, and the squares larger, than the men's, and put me in mind of the ancient Picts. This serves them for a veil, and covers both head and body. The men wear theirs after another manner, expecially when designed for ornament it is loose and flowing, like the mantles our painters give their heroes. Their thighs are bare, with brawny muscles. Nature had drawn all her strokes bold and masterly, what is covered is only adapted to necessity – their brogue on the foot, a short buskin of various colours on the legg, tied above the calf with a striped pair of garters. What should be concealed is hid with a large shot-pouch, on each side of which hangs a pistol and a dagger, as if they found it necessary to keep these parts well guarded. A round target on their back, a blew bonnet on their heads, in one hand a broad sword, and a musquet in the other; perhaps no nation goes better armed . . .

The evolution of the tartan and the plaid is shown in illustrations from the 16th century onwards. In a map of Scotland by John Speed, who lived from 1552-1629, there is a coloured illustration showing a belted plaid in red and blue stripes on white (and probably undyed) wool, and in Blaeu's map of Scotland, the *Scotia Antiqua* of 1643, there are pictures of Scots wearing belted plaids and trews and circular, flat bonnets. Hieronymous Tielssch's travel album of the same period shows a man in a tartan belted plaid edged with brown fur and a woman wearing a cloak in a yellow and blue tartan with red lines, clasped by fine brooches. There is also a German woodcut of 1631 showing Scottish soldiers wearing what appear to be tartan plaids adapted to a Continental style of dress.

During the century leading up to the Jacobite uprising of 1745, the development of the tartan can also be seen in paintings. In the portrait of the Highland Chieftain, possibly Lord Breadalbane, by Michael Wright circa 1660, which hangs in the National Portrait Gallery in Edinburgh, the neatly arranged belted plaid is in several shades of brown and red with black and crimson stripes, but it does not have a regular sett or repeat. His silk-embroidered doublet is repeatedly slashed to show a full, white frilled shirt, and his red hose with black dicing has a horizontal seam above the calf and a 'cock's comb' running down the vertical seam at the back of the leg. The hose is gartered with large gold ribbons and his flat brogues have ankle straps and large tongues. His wide bonnet is decorated with a large ostrich plume. Thus the chieftain is dressed in the typical court costume of the day.

Besides Wright's unknown chieftain, there are a number of other paintings of the 17th and early 18th centuries showing Highland nobility in Scottish dress. From the point of view of the tartan, probably the most significant are those by Richard Waitt, who painted some twelve portraits for the Clan Grant in the first quarter of the 18th century. They include Patrick Grant of Miltown, John Grant of Burnside, Alasdair Grant the Champion and William Grant the Piper, all of whom, except the Champion and the Piper, wear different colours and setts of tartans: Patrick Grant, for example, has a plaid in green and red with black lines and John Grant a plaid in yellow, blue and white with red lines.

However, what is also significant about the Clan Grant is that in 1703 the Laird of Grant ordered 'tartan coats all of one colour and style' – red and green – for his 600 men-at-

Portrait of a Highland Chieftain, possibly Lord Breadalbane, painted by Michael Wright circa 1660.

arms. But what he did not specify was a 'Clan Grant' tartan. Surely, had there been one, he would have demanded it. In fact, in none of the portraits at Castle Grant are the tartans repeated, nor do they relate to the Grant tartan of today. Waitt would have displayed an extensive collection of ready-painted, tartan-clad 'bodies' from which a client could select the pose and tartan of his or her choice, whereupon the head would be added to complete the portrait.

The argument against there being specific clan tartans in the 18th century seems even more convincing if we look at the protrait of Andrew MacPherson, 19th Chief of the Clan Chattan, who was painted by an unknown artist. The Chief is wearing jacket, trews and plaid, but the jacket is in deep green with reddish-brown stripes and blue horizontal lines, the trews are in green with brownish-blue stripes, and the plaid in a lighter green with orange and white stripes and red lines. Thus he is, in effect, wearing three different tartans. Furthermore, the positioning of the plaid shows a difference in thread count between warp and weft which is quite unlike the balanced design of the modern clan tartan. It confirms both Sir Walter Scott's remark in a letter written to his friend Mrs Hughes following her query about clan tartans and their origins that

> I do not believe a word of the nonsense about every clan or name having a regular pattern which was undeviatingly adhered to . . .

and D. W. Stewart's comment in his article on tartans in *Family Portraits:*

> A careful study of these, and of examples of tartan fabrics which can be proved to date from the risings of 1715 and 1745, reveals the fact that almost all the tartans differ from those in present use.

The first half of the 18th century saw a turbulent period in Scottish history which culminated in the Jacobite uprising of 1745, when Prince Charles Edward Stuart arrived from exile in France to claim the British throne. Prince Charles was the grandson of James II, the last Stuart King of England and Scotland who fled to France in 1688, and his campaign was at first successful, since he not only regained Scotland but led his Scottish army south of the border into England where George II had already packed his bags and was ready to flee to the Continent. However, after Prince Charles' appointment of the Irishman O'Sullivan to lead his army in preference to Lord George Murray, who was undoubtedly the best general in the land, the cohesion of the Jacobite forces began to break down. This is, of course, a very simplified generalization about an extremely complicated situation, but given better leadership it seems that Prince Charles might have gained the British crown for the House of Stewart. For a fuller picture, it is worth reading more; for example *Charles Edward Stuart – the man, the king, the legend* by Hugh Douglas and *Culloden* by John Prebble.

The Jacobite uprising was finally crushed by the Duke of Cumberland at the Battle of Culloden in Invernesshire in 1746 where the Scottish army of 5,000 Highlanders was routed by the superior leadership and strategy of the English forces (which incidentally had many Scots in their ranks). For Prince Charles, it meant flight from the east to the west of Scotland, and his final return to France from Loch Nam Uamh, Invernesshire. But for the rest of his Highland countrymen, it meant not only the destruction of the clan system, but also the banning of the Highland dress (and thus the tartan).

There is evidence that, during the battle, the tartan did little to help distinguish one side from another and that the Duke, seeing a wounded Highlander on the battlefield, had to ask which side he was on before ordering him to be shot – an order which a Major James Wolfe refused to obey. (He was the same Wolfe who, thirteen years later, was to lead Scottish soldiers against the French in Canada. Then, he said taking Scots to Canada would help solve the 'Highland problem', and that it did not matter if they never returned home.) As a Highland officer noted in *A Journal of the Expedition of Prince Charles Edward in 1745*,

> We M'Donalds were much perplex'd, in the event of ane ingagement, how to distinguish ourselves from our brethen and neighbours the M'Donalds of Sky, seeing we were both Highlanders and both wore heather in our bonnets, only our white cockades made some distinction.

But the tartan did give Prince Charles a new identity – and indeed immediately became associated with his cause. The Jacobite historian, Miss Henrietta Taylor, who has researched the Stuart papers at Windsor Castle, says that

> when the Prince first put on the kilt, he leapt in the air and said that now he "only required to have the itch to become a complete Highlander"

and there are a number of pictures showing Prince Charles in Highland garb, including a miniature presented by the Prince to the 'Gentle Lochiel' showing him wearing a tartan coat and a flat bonnet with a white cockade. A similar portrait in the National Portrait Gallery in Edinburgh shows the Prince wearing a tartan that has red and black stripes on a white line (and is unlike any modern tartan), and in another in the Dhuleep Singh Collection the Prince is wearing a bright blue bonnet and a tartan jacket consisting of a red ground, green stripes and yellow lines.

There are also many pieces of tartan which are said to have been worn by Prince Charles, usually at Culloden. Among them is a complete costume at the United Service Museum in Edinburgh which consists of a coat made of hard tartan with a purple collar with deep cuffs, and two side pockets with large flaps. It has mushroom-shaped bone buttons with silver inlays bearing the Stuart rose and nine green thread button hoops. The trews are made up of several pieces of tartan sewn together and are a simple green and red checked pattern cut in a way to run diagonally across the leg. From a distance, the jacket appears striped rather than checked because the threads of the weft are beaten closely together and therefore dominate those of the warp. The order of the weft also differs slightly from that

DETAIL FROM P. D. MORIER'S PAINTING OF THE BATTLE OF CULLODEN, 1746.

of the warp and is clearly a mid-18th century pattern.

One of the pieces of tartan said to have been worn by the Prince was obtained by Bishop Robert Forbes, an enthusiastic Jacobite who collected mementoes of Prince Charles Edward. A note by Bishop Forbes under a fragment of tartan with a bit of red lining reads:

> The above are pieces of the outside and inside of that identical waistcoat which Macdonald of Kingsburgh gave to the Prince when he laid aside the woman's clothes. The said waistcoat being too fine for a servant, the Prince exchanged it with Malcolm Macleod. Malcolm, after parting with the Prince, and finding himself in danger of being seized, did hide the waistcoat in a cleft of rock, where, upon his returning home in the beginning of September 1747, he found it all rotten to bits, except only as much as would serve to cover little more than one's loof, and two buttons, all of which he was pleased to send to me. The waistcoat had lain more than a full year in the cleft of the rock, for Malcolm Macleod was made prisoner sometime in 1746.

To the Government in London the Jacobite uprising was the last straw. There had already been attempts to curb the warlike activities of the Highlanders and their barbaric nature with, for example, a Disarming Act of 1725, and in 1746 a new Disarming Act was passed which proscribed the wearing of Highland dress, an action which Henry VIII had previously taken against the Irish. The first target of the Proscription was Prince Charles himself, who was shown in innumerable caricatures wearing Highland dress. Perhaps the most famous was one entitled 'A likeness notwithstanding the disguise that any person who secures the Son of the Pretender is intitled to a reward of £30,000.' But, equally, the Proscription was intended to destroy the political and racial symbolism of the tartan High-

AN ILLUSTRATION, ABOVE, OF THE STORY TOLD BY
SIR PHILIP JENNING CLERKE OF HOW THE WIFE OF A HAMPSHIRE INNKEEPER AND THEIR
DAUGHTERS COULD NOT KEEP THEIR EYES OFF HIGHLAND OFFICERS CLAD IN HIGHLAND DRESS.
RIGHT, PORTRAIT OF PRINCE CHARLES EDWARD STUART BY JOHN PETTIE.

land dress – and to destroy any notion that the Highlanders might have had that they were different (and separate) from subjects in the rest of the British Kingdom. Thus any Highlander whose loyalty was suspect was made to take the following oath:

> I, ————, do swear, and as I shall have to answer to God at the Great Day of Judgement, I shall not nor shall have in my possession any gun, sword, pistol or arm whatsoever; and never use any tartan, plaid or any part of the Highland garb; and if I do so, may I be cursed in my undertakings, family and property – may I never see my wife and children, father, mother and relations – may I be killed in battle as a coward, and lie without Christain burial, in a strange land, far from the graves of my forefathers and kindred; may all this come across me if I break my oath.

Rather illogically, it did *not* apply to the Highland Regiments, women, or landowners and sons of landowners: it was assumed that all Jacobite landowners had either been killed or had fled to France, and that all the others were loyal to George II.

The Proscription was a terrible burden to place on a proud race, and even more terrible because, for the first few years of its enforcement, troops were ordered 'to kill upon the spot any person whom they met dressed in the Highland garb.' Given that many ordinary Highlanders spoke only Gaelic, and might never even hear of the Act if they lived in remote areas, it was just as well that its strict enforcement was not maintained for long, and that, following a campaign by the Highland Society of London, the Act was repealed in 1782 by a Bill introduced by John Graham, Marquis of Graham (later the Duke of Montrose) in the House of Commons on 17 June. A Gaelic proclamation declared:

> Eiso! Eiso!
> Listen men! This is bringing before all the Sons of Gael that the king and Parliament of Britain have forever abolished the Act against the Highland dress that came down to the Clans from the beginning of the world to the year 1746. This must bring great joy to every Highland heart. You are no longer bound down to the unmanly dress of the Lowlander. This is declaring to every man, young and old, simple and gentle, that they may after this put on and wear the trews, the little kilt, doublet and hose, along with the belted plaid, without fear of the law of the land or the spite of enemies.

But the Bill was not passed without opposition. Parliamentary records note that

> Sir Philip Jennings Clerke said he would oppose the bill when brought in, if it did not confine the Highland dress to the North of the Tweed; for he recollected an innkeeper in Hampshire coming with a complaint before him as justice of the peace, that four Highland officers were quartered on him, who being brawny, handsome fellows, he began to be jealous of his wife, who was not very old, and also fearful for the virtue of his daughters; the Highlanders, being in their own country dress, the females could not keep their eyes off them, which obliged him to take a lodging for them near his house, but far from being able to attend his business, his whole time was taken up with watching his wife and daughters.

The long years of the ban had their effect. Defeat at Culloden began a cycle of depopulation in the Highlands, with people being driven out of their homes, or leaving in despair, usually to emigrate overseas. The continuity in the development of the Highland dress (and the tartan) had been broken, as Dr Samuel Johnson noted after his tour of the Highlands in 1783:

> The law by which the Highlanders have been obliged to change the form of their dress has, in all the places that we have visited, been universally obeyed. I have seen only one gentleman completely clothed in the ancient habit, and by him it was worn only occasionally and wantonly.

In the years following the repeal of the Proscription, there were three major developments in the readoption of the Highland dress and the tartan. The first was the move to establish a clearer link between specific tartans and individual clans – a move which was eventually to lead, 180 years later, to the setting up of the present Scottish Tartans Society in 1963. The second was the widespread use of the small kilt – the *feileadh-beag* or *filibeg* – which has now become the norm for male Highland dress. And the third was the adoption of Highland dress by Lowland Scots – i.e. those living outside the Highland area – a development which rapidly spread south of the Scottish border, and of course applied to Scots living overseas.

With regard to the link between tartans and specific clans, this goes back to the documentary records of William Wilson & Son of Bannockburn, near Stirling, a company which was probably the most successful of all the commercial tartan weavers and was in business from 1720-1976. Its first sketchy records date from the 1780s, i.e. the years immediately following the repeal of the Proscription, and by 1819 it had a list of several scores of tartans with full weaving particulars. The clans or names to which they were said to belong were Aberdeen, Birral, Baillie, Old Bruce, New Bruce (neither of which, as Donald Stewart points out in his article in the *Proceedings of the Scottish Tartans Society, No 1 1975,* resembles the modern Clan Bruce tartan), Caledonia, Crieff, Dundee, Gordon (this was not the regimental sett), Gallowater, Hunt, Lochaber, Lasting, Logan, Fort William, Perth, Ritch and Waggrall. None of these is now a clan sett except New Bruce, which is sold as a Drummond or a Grant, and Caledonian, which is the (red) clan MacPherson.

The truth is that at the end of the 18th century, the situation was so chaotic that Wilsons simply had to provide tartans as best they could. At first, demand was weak and money short, so that the company noted that most requests for tartans were limited to 'Logan setts', 'Gordons with silk' and 'course kilts with red'. One customer said: 'The colours I leave to yourself and let them be handsome.' Wilsons were also facing stiff competition from weavers in Norwich, East Anglia, and a Scottish customer complained that the Norwich manufacturers 'add only a penny for the same quantity of that colour (red) for which you charge 6d.' The red line was being added to a tartan 'to brighten it up'.

However, within 30 years or so the situation was vastly different, and after George IV visited Scotland in 1822, Messrs J. Spittal & Son of Edinburgh were writing to Wilsons saying, 'We are like to be torn to pieces for tartan, the demand is so great we cannot supply our customers.' The visit of George IV – the first British monarch to travel north of the Border since Charles II's departure from Scotland in 1651 – provided the occasion for a gathering of the Clans, with groups of Clansmen, each headed by its chief, in their 'ancestral clan tartan', and the King in the full Highland dress shown in the portrait by Sir David Wilkie (and less flatteringly in innumerable cartoons of the day). The gathering was the idea of General David Stewart of Garth, a notable Highland enthusiast, and it led to a colossal demand for tartans which Wilsons could only meet by installing an extra 40 looms in their weaving sheds to satisfy requests for 'the truest pattern of the Murray' and 'the real

CARTOON SHOWING GEORGE IV AND ALDERMAN SIR WILLIAM CURTIS IN EDINBURGH IN 1822.

Ross' – tartans which were often supplied after scouring the Highlands for old patterns which were at first numbered and then randomly associated with clan names.

There was also an attempt by the London Highland Society to bring some order into the situation and from 1815 onwards, Clan Chiefs were asked to provide the Society with samples of their clan tartans. This a number of Chiefs did – whether or not they knew what their clan tartans really were – but over the years the specimens have been greatly reduced in size (so that they may not show a complete sett) and now languish in a London vault. Thus even their value as evidence of what people thought the clan tartans were during the early part of the 19th century has been greatly diminished. Another important effort at research was also made by James Logan, who spent several years visiting places in Scotland where tartan was woven, notably in the Stirling area, and met in Bannockburn an old man known as 'the Lord Lyon of Tartan heraldry' (see pages 178 & 179 for the role of Lord Lyon King of Arms with regard to tartans). The result was Logan's book, *The Scottish Gael,* which was published in 1831 and recorded 55 different setts, each of which was accurately described.

However, when it comes to the story of hunting down 'authentic' tartans, nothing is as amazing as the appearance of two brothers, John and Charles Allan, who arrived in Scotland claiming to be the grandsons of Prince Charles Edward and thus the legitimate heirs of the House of Stewart. Not only that, but they then produced a tattered and battered-looking manuscript of 38 pages bearing the date 1721 which they claimed was a careless 18th-century transcript of a manuscript dating from before 1571. This, they said, had previously belonged to Prince Charles and before him to John, Bishop of Ross. Only the transcript, now known as the *Cromarty MS,* has ever been seen (its predecessor, the *Douai MS,* was never produced), and it contained brief descriptions of some 75 tartans, written in plausible 16th-century Scots. It was this manuscript that a friend of the two brothers, Sir Thomas Dick Lauder, transcribed into modern English. Then, in June 1829, Charles Allan added pages showing the clans or families, each with pseudo-heraldic devices, and water-colour drawings of the tartans according to the *Cromarty MS* descriptions. This particular version, known as the *Lauder Transcript,* is now in the Royal Library at Windsor. And by

A SELF-PORTRAIT BY JOHN AND CHARLES SOBIESKI STUART, PRETENDERS TO THE SCOTTISH THRONE, PAINTED AT EILEAN AIGAS, THE HOUSE GIVEN TO THEM BY LORD LOVAT WHEN THEY SETTLED ON HIS ESTATES.

this time, the fame of the two brothers had become enhanced by their assumption of the name Sobieski, which was that of the Polish Royal family to which Prince Charles Edward's mother belonged. John Allan was even signing himself 'John Sobieski Stuart'.

From the start, serious misgivings had been expressed about the authenticity of the *Cromarty MS*. Sir Walter Scott, responsible more than anyone else for the rehabilitation of Scotland's reputation after the disastrous defeat at Culloden, declared it to be spurious in both content and language. But that did not prevent Sir Thomas and Charles Allan publishing the *Lauder Transcript* together with the family heraldry and illustrations of tartans, as the *Vestiarium Scoticum*. As Donald Stewart says,

> The *Vestiarium* proved a godsend to the tartan trade. The descriptions in the text were far from precise, but it was easy enough for the weavers to follow the illustrations; where these departed in colour from the text, it was these, not the text, that served as the model. Soon these reputedly

ancient tartans became very popular, and many of the clan tartans of today have no previous authority, yet meet with the full approval of most (but not all) of the respective Clan Chiefs.

Since the publication of the *Vestiarium Scoticum* in 1842, the *Cromarty MS* from which it was derived has been subjected to chemical analysis (in 1896) to prove that at least its dating back to 1721 was genuine (the results were said to be non-conclusive), while *photographic prints* of the MS have been analysed by philologists including J. Charles Thompson of Arlington, DC, who made an almost complete transcript of the text in the 1920s from which he concluded that the *Cromarty MS* was spurious: according to him its words and syntax were either extinct before the supposed date of the *Douai MS* or not yet in use when *Cromarty MS* was supposed to be written. Similarly, in the book *Scotland's Forged Tartans* Donald Stewart has analysed the tartans described in the *Vestiarium Scoticum* and concludes that 'many of the tartans, never before recorded, carried a strange resemblance to the tartans of the same name in current use about 1829.'

The second major development in Scottish dress following the lifting of the Proscription in 1782 was the growing popularity of the small kilt and, like the supposed authenticity of many 'clan tartans', this was also subject to myth and misunderstanding. There is some evidence, for example, that the small kilt was introduced by an Englishman called Thomas Rawlinson who smelted iron in Glengarry in the 1730s. One story says that Rawlinson, who wore the Highland dress himself, noted the inconvenience of being unable to remove the upper half of the *feileadh breacan* (tartan plaid) when it became soaked in the rain without removing the lower part too, and another story says that he invented the little kilt because the full plaid made it difficult for his men to work in his smelting works in reasonable safety. Whatever the truth of these stories, Rawlinson's example was followed by Iain MacDonnel, who became Chief of Glengarry in 1720. And the earliest known illustration of the little kilt probably appears in the portrait of his son, Alasdair Ruadh MacDonnel, The Young Glengarry, painted after his release from the Tower of London in 1747, where the little kilt is worn by the retainer in the background.

The adoption of the small kilt coincided with the replacement of the doublet by the short tartan coat, the *cota goirid*. The earliest illustration of this particular garment occurs in the portrait of James Fraser of Castle Leathers of 1723. He wears a jacket of a simple tartan underneath which is a waistcoat of the same tartan trimmed at the cuffs in gold. The same tartan is also used for his trews which have red garters just below the knee. Gartering in this fashion was adopted to reduce the tension in the cloth at the knee. James Fraser also has a leather pouch (sporran?) with two red cords and buff tassels, a scarlet shoulder plaid (though it is so small it hardly seems a plaid at all), a varnished leather strap over his right shoulder and a blue bonnet with a black cockade. The cockade shows his loyalty to the House of Hanover. A black stock, frilled and ruffled shirt, and square-toed shoes complete this rather fanciful outfit.

The Fraser portrait is also notable for being the earliest in oils to depict trews. Like the little kilt, trews were becoming increasingly popular just before the Jacobite uprising of 1745. As Martin Martin wrote in 1703:

> Many people wear trowes, some of them very fine woven, like stockings of those made of cloth; some are coloured and others are striped; the latter are well shaped like the former, lying close to the body from the middle downwards, tied round with a belt above the Haunches.

The third major development in the use of the tartan following the lifting of the Proscription in 1782 was its adoption beyond the Highlands. With the encouragement of the re-

Major Fraser of Castle Leathers, wearing a short coat, waistcoat and trews all in the same tartan, a leather pouch and a tartan plaid. Artist unknown.

The drawing room at Balmoral, designed by Prince Albert, who covered walls, floors and furniture in tartan. Not to mention retainers of the Royal Family, who were dressed in Balmoral tartan.

building of the clans by people like General David Stewart of Garth, it is not surprising that tartans spread to the Lowlands of Scotland. But it was a development that did not occur without comment. As Sir Walter Scott wrote in a letter to Sir Thomas Dick Lauder (of the *Lauder Transcript*) on 19 November 1829:

> To suppose Lowlanders to be Highlanders we must suppose that they spoke the Gaelick, and held the system of clanship. Without this, there could be no occasion for wearing clan tartans. Now, every law or regulation concerning clanship is limited to the Highlands and to the Borders, who seem to have it as a tie of communication calculated to bind a tribe strongly together. But we are now required to believe that there was none of that distinction of dress at all, and if not of dress, why should there be any difference of language or laws? A nation's dress is much more easily changed than its manners and language. The idea of distinguishing the clans by their tartans is but a fashion of modern date.

But Sir Walter also recognized, in an earlier letter to Sir Thomas (dated 5 June 1829), that the use of tartans in the Lowlands probably began with the Union of Scotland and England in 1707, 'when the detestation of that measure led it to be adopted as the national colour, and the ladies all affected tartan screens or mantles.' The Lowlands also adopted what has become known as a 'Shepherd's Tartan' of small checks of blue, black, green or brown on a light ground, worn very much in the fashion of earlier Highland dress as a wrap in bad weather. In fine weather, it was drawn around the wait or worn gracefully over the left shoulder.

South of the Border, the revival in tartans was encouraged long before George IV arrived in Edinburgh in 1822. As early as 1792, Jane Maxwell, Duchess of Gordon, better known as the 'Tartan Belle', introduced a plaid woven in the tartan of the Black Watch to the English court to celebrate her son's appointment to that regiment. The Gordon tartan followed a year later. Not surprisingly, it was based upon the Black Watch pattern. And from London, the fashion travelled to Paris. It became especially popular in 1815 when Scottish troops occupied Paris during the Napoleonic war.

George IV's visit was, of course, of crucial importance in the re-establishment of the tartan, as were the activities of the Allan brothers already mentioned. But the final seal of approval undoubtedly came from Queen Victoria whose love of Scotland led to her introducing Prince Albert to the country in 1842. They first used the Balmoral estate as the Royal summer residence in 1848, and subsequently bought it in 1852. The Prince Consort, being not only a man of letters, but also a scientist, an architect and a designer, was then inspired to invent the Balmoral tartan, which includes unusual yarns composed of different ratios of black and white threads, representing the subtle greys of the Deeside granites. It was woven in a heavy cloth for the royal ghillies and in a softer version on a dove-grey ground for the Royal Family. By the time the Prince Consort had finished rebuilding Balmoral Castle, its floors, furniture and walls (not to mention inhabitants) were covered in tartan.

Thus, in the history of cloth, not only is there nothing to compare with the myths, romantic associations and bloodshed associated with tartans: there is also no other cloth whose fortunes have been so closely connected with royal families – with the ill-fated House of Stewart, whose claim to the British throne lies with the Comte de Paris; with the German House of Hanover; and with the current House of Windsor, which still maintains the royal interest. There are still tartans exclusive to the Royal Family, including the Balmoral already mentioned, and the Lord of the Isles and the Duke of Rothesay, which is only worn by Prince Charles (see page 163).

The control of tartans, such as it is, now rests with three authorities: the Clan Chiefs, Lord Lyon King of Arms, and the Scottish Tartans Society, whose respective roles are described later in this book. Not only do they have to advise on the wearing of tartans and the authenticity of patterns past and present, but they are also called upon to comment upon tartans which are designed today, since the demand for new tartans remains as great as it was 150 years ago, and they continue to be worn by Scots both at home and abroad. The enduring affection people have for the tartan has remained as strong as ever: there is no reason to suppose it will not continue to do so.

TWO BALMORAL KEEPERS, DONALD STEWART AND CHARLES DUNCAN.

THE WEAVE

The structure of a woven cloth affects its performance: the way in which the warp and weft interlace (the 'weave') influences the flexibility of the cloth and the way it drapes or hangs. It also determines the strength of the fabric, and how it will withstand abrasion in everyday wear, and also snagging (which can lead to broken threads and a spoiled surface).

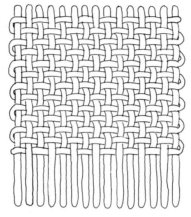

PLAIN WEAVE

The simplest of all weaves is called 'plain weave' which is a basic over-one, under-one interlacement. It is the strongest weave, because of the maximum number of intersections of warp and weft. It also needs less yarn than cloths of other weaves. This is not always an advantage, however, and certainly when planning a cloth for a garment such as a plaid, or the later kilt, a flexible but heavy-weight cloth (i.e. containing more yarn than is possible with plain weave) would be desirable. The 2 × 2 twill weave is ideal for this purpose – its regular over-two, under-two interlacement, moving sideways one thread with every weft 'pick' produces a visible small diagonal rib, and a very flexible cloth, which when woven in a good worsted yarn will produce a heavy 'hard' tartan ideal for a kilt, and responsible for its comfort and 'swing'.

2 × 2 TWILL WEAVE

Other twill weaves would not have been used because their interlacing (e.g. 2 × 1, 1 × 2, 3 × 1 or 1 × 3) is unbalanced, so that in a checked fabric the colours would be emphasized in one way only, spoiling the desired effect. The next balanced twill available is the 3 × 3, and this would not be possible to weave on the 4-shaft looms of the Highlands.

Sometimes a tartan cloth is woven in plain weave, where this is more suitable for the purpose: the traditional diagonal-cut neck-tie, for example, is often made of plain weave tartan, as a twill cloth, cut on the bias, can often be *too* flexible, and leads to bagging on the surface. Commercially woven tartan tie cloths in plain weave are usually woven with a 'miniature' tartan sett adapted by making some stripes narrower so that a smaller pattern repeat is obtained.

BALANCE

When a tartan cloth is planned, the warp and weft must have the same number of ends and picks per inch/cm. This is known as a 'balanced' cloth, and is essential so that both warp and weft colours can be equally emphasized, and to ensure that the check design remains square.

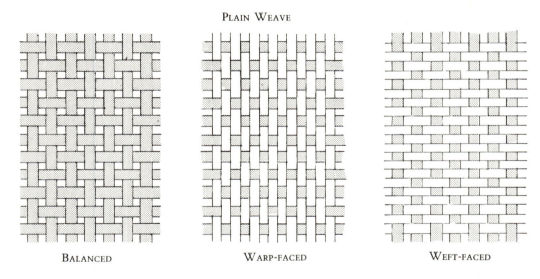

PLAIN WEAVE

BALANCED   WARP-FACED   WEFT-FACED

<blockquote>

The black go by the white thread,
The white go by the black led,
The green go in between red,
The red between the black thread.

The black go in between red,
The red between the white thread,
The white between the green led,
The green between the white thread.

The white between the blue thread,
The blue between the bright red,
The blue, the scarlet hue thread,
The scarlet true the due thread.

The scarlet to the blue thread,
The blue to scarlet hue wed,
The scarlet to the black led,
The black unto the bright red.

A thread go to the threads two,
Of colours two, good and true,
The two the threads of black due,
The one the thread of white through.

Seven threads to five be,
And five be unto three,
Three to two, two to one,
In every border done.

</blockquote>

(Song describing tartan sett – from Benbecula, Outer Hebridies)

SETT AND SCALE

SETT

The usual meaning of 'sett' in weaving is to describe the numbers of warp and weft threads in an inch/cm. The same yarn can be 'sett' in many ways: a very close sett will produce a stiff heavy fabric; a very open sett will give a soft loose cloth. Often something between the two is desirable: the 'sett' of the yarn, in relationship to the weave used, is a vital part of all woven textile design and performance.

In the study and weaving of tartans, however, the word 'sett' has an additional meaning: the proportion and distribution of the coloured stripes in the warp (to be repeated in the weft) which distinguishes one tartan from another.

RED	12	12			4		8
GREEN		6					
BLUE			2		2	16	
WHITE				2			

CAMERON OF LOCHIEL

SCALE

The 'sett' (colour distribution) is stated not in numbers of threads, but in numbers denoting proportion. It will be seen that the lowest of these is 2. No stripe is less than that number because the shuttle containing the weft thread must pass backwards and forwards across the cloth, to return to the same selvedge. This striping in pairs of threads is a restriction of many power-looms, but has always been used by handweavers especially when weaving 2 × 2 twill cloths, as the twill repeats in four 'treadlings', and the use of colours in twos and multiples of two ensures that fewer mistakes are made. It is easier to count whilst weaving, and helps the weaver to weave faster and with an even rhythm (especially valuable when weaving tartan cloth). These numbers in the tartan setts can be multiplied by any amount if a larger repeat is desired when using a fine thread. They must never be divided, however. It will be obvious that the size of the minimum repeat will therefore vary greatly from tartan to tartan: the MacGregor Rob Roy could be any size from 4 threads upwards (but is often shown as a 1-inch check) whereas the complicated Ogilvie of Airlie with its minimum of 862 threads in a repeat would have needed to have been sett at 32 warp ends per inch in order that one repeat could be woven on the 27-inch width cloth which is the traditional cloth width for handwoven fabric.

The scale of the tartan is determined, then,
a) by the size of the particular tartan 'sett', or 'repeat',
b) by the count (or thickness) of the yarn,
c) by the sett (ends/picks per inch/cm) of the threads.

TARTAN IN DIFFERENT SIZES FOR USE AS TRAVEL RUG AND DRESS FABRIC.

THE YARN AND SPINNING

Traditionally, tartans are woven in an all-wool yarn. Wool fibres can be treated in two different ways before spinning, however, and this treatment affects the appearance and performance of the fabric. In tartan, these two wool cloths are referred to as 'hard' and 'soft'.

HARD TARTANS are woven from worsted wool. The fibres are combed into alignment before being spun into a yarn: the resulting yarn is smooth and 'cool' and will weave into a crisp-looking and heavy wool cloth, ideal for the traditional kilt.

SOFT TARTANS are woven from woollen-spun yarns, in which the wool fibres are brushed, or carded, so that they lie at right angles to one another. When spun, the yarn is springy, and holds pockets of air, making the resulting cloth warmer in use, with a slightly fuzzy appearance and soft to handle.

Both of these fibre preparation processes can be used prior to either hand- or machine-spinning.

Many other fibres are used for weaving tartans: both silk and cotton for lighter weight cloth have been popular for over a century. In the past, tartan seems to have varied greatly in weight, weave and fibre: in 1831 the Edinburgh merchants Romanes & Patterson ('Scottish Tartan, Shawl & Silk Warehouse') stocked tartans in 'Worsted, Silk and Worsted, Sarsenet, Satin and Tweeled Silk' and also in 'Tabbinet, Spun Silk, Velvet, and Superfine Worsted'. (Readers who are familiar with cloth structure will be puzzled at the inclusion of 'Satin' and 'Velvet', as both of these weaves produce cloths in which colour is shown in warp stripes only, whereas tartan demands that exactly equal quantities of warp and weft are visible.)

WOOL

Until the middle of the 18th century the wool used in the Highlands came from the now extinct Highland sheep. This was a small animal, naturally short-tailed, probably horned in the male and polled in the female. It was naturally wool-shedding, and multi-coloured, although white would have been favoured because of the problem of obtaining bright colours in dyeing on a coloured fleece. Their fine fibres were plucked, or gathered when shed, not shorn as are those of other sheep, and they could be spun into a soft but firm worsted yarn of fine quality. The introduction of the Scottish Blackface with its harder springy fleece (now used mainly for good quality carpets), meant that interbreeding took place and the wool quality changed. Cheviot sheep were also introduced from the Lowlands and Borders, and it soon became impossible to spin the crisp fine worsted yarn with indigenous fleece. The worsted yarn which is used today for weaving good tartan cloth is spun mainly from New Zealand cross-bred fleece.

Far left; Black-faced mountain sheep — in 1890 they made up 70% of the sheep in Scotland.
Left; Cheviot sheep — introduced into the Highlands from the Lowlands and Borders.
Above; Shetland and Orkney sheep — closely related to the extinct Highland sheep.

PREPARING THE FIBRES FOR SPINNING

After wool fibres have been shorn (or, sometimes, plucked) from the sheep, there are several stages of processing before they can be spun into a yarn, whether by hand or by machine. A well-shorn fleece can be unrolled like a sheepskin, and laid out for sorting. Not all parts of the sheep's wool are of equal quality. The finest fibres are at the front end of the sheep, mainly on the shoulders (called 'diamond') and the fibres on the back of the sheep are usually short and dry, because the rain will have washed the natural oil towards the sides of the animal. The fibres on the back legs (called 'britch') will often be coarse and 'hairy'. The different qualities will spin into different types of yarn, and most hand-spinners will want to do this. As well as the varying qualities of fibre within one fleece, the different breeds of sheep produce very different types of fibre. Those with long fibres usually have their fleece spun into worsted yarn, and those with short crinkly fibres are useful for woollen yarn spinning.

PREPARATION FOR WORSTED SPINNING

In the Highlands, most old tartans would be called 'hard', and would have been woven from worsted spun yarn. The long fine fleece from the old Highland sheep would have been plucked, or gathered, and then drawn, in handfuls, through metal spikes, set into a head like a coarse comb. This comb would be heated, to soften the natural lanolin in the fibres, and to help to straighten them, because the object in preparing fibres for worsted spinning is to get them straight and parallel, so that the yarn spun from them is cool, smooth and lustrous, with no projecting fibres.

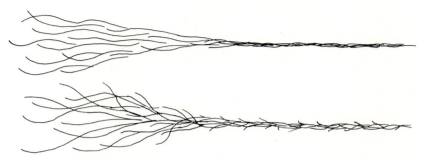

WOOLLEN FIBRES BECOMING YARN. TOP; WORSTED SPUN   BOTTOM; WOOLLEN SPUN

PREPARATION FOR WOOLLEN SPINNING

The object in preparing fibres for being spun 'woollen' is to get the fibres lying at right angles to one another, so that when they are spun they make a 'full' yarn, which will hold pockets of air, and be elastic and springy. In the Highlands, wool for knitting would be spun in this way, and so would the wool for weaving 'soft' tartan.

For woollen spinning, the fibres are first teased apart, so that pieces of twig and other unwanted matter will fall out. The teased fibres are then spread over 'carders' – for hand-spinning, these look like rectangular bats with one side covered with a surface of hooked wires. The fibres are transferred from one carder to another until evenly brushed into a light fluffy mass. This is in the form of a roll, or 'rolag', for hand-spinning, and the fibres are taken from the end of the roll to feed into the twist, so that they remain at right angles to one another: the opposite of worsted spinning.

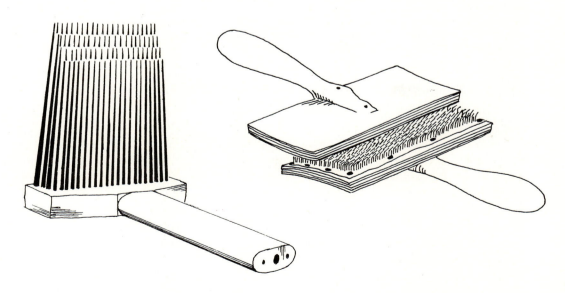

ABOVE RIGHT; CARDERS, FOR PREPARATION OF FIBRES: WOOLLEN SPINNING,
ABOVE LEFT; COMBS, FOR PREPARATION OF FIBRES: WORSTED SPINNING
RIGHT; WOOL FIBRES BEING CARDED IN A MODERN MILL.

SPINNING

In order that individual fibres can be turned into a yarn, capable of withstanding the further processes of weaving or knitting, a certain amount of twist must be given to them. The amount imparted will vary according to the fibre, and the end use of the yarn, but the ways of twisting the fibres, and thus spinning a yarn, is basically the same, (with only minor variations) all over the world.

One of the simplest, and oldest, tools in the world is the drop-spindle (Gaelic: *fearsaid*). This consists of a stick, usually 10-12 inches long and notched at the top, with a weight, or whorl, at the other end. This whorl can be made of wood, horn, clay or stone, and spindle whorls dating back to the Iron Age have been found all over Scotland. Spindles have also been found where the stick itself is shaped with a wider, heavier end to act as a whorl. Occasionally, a small potato would have been pushed on to a stick to act as a whorl. The spindle was a cheap tool, easy to make, carry and store. With practice, it is possible to spin a fine and even thread on it. The prepared fleece would have been attached to a distaff, and carried in one arm, while the spindle was twisted and dropped with the other hand, drawing more strands of fleece from the distaff, and putting twist in them to make the yarn, which was then strong enough to support the next drop of the spindle as the process was repeated. Occasionally the spinner would wind the completed yarn on to the spindle shaft to store it before spinning another length. As this length was dependent on the amount of drop available, spindle-spinning was practised while standing up, or even walking or riding about. Although a slow process, it could be done while herding cattle, or minding sheep, and so it was a popular method of spinning even after spinning wheels became universally available, in the early 19th century.

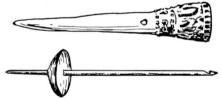

Two types of drop-spindle

The first wheel to be introduced to the Highlands (in the early 18th century) was the 'muckle-wheel', or spindle wheel (called a Great Wheel in Lowland Scotland). This was far from portable, being a simple arrangement of a large fly-wheel mounted vertically over a board and connected by a single driving band to a pointed spindle. This spindle was mounted horizontally in bearings which were often made of straw, because of its naturally slippery surface. The wheel was turned by hand, with the fibres attached to the spindle which twisted them into a yarn. The spinner would gradually draw them away from the spindle end, at a slight angle. The required amount of twist could be imparted, then the spun yarn was wound on to the spindle from the side, to store it in a ball until a quantity was ready. This process was then repeated, and could become almost continuous when practised by a skilled spinner. These wheels could also be used for winding the bobbins of weft yarn for the weavers' shuttles, and continued to be used for that purpose when they had been superseded by the 'flyer' or 'saxony' wheel.

The flyer wheel is familiar today as the one which is used for the craft of hand-spinning. It has a much smaller wheel than the 'muckle-wheel', set either alongside the spindle or directly below it. (There is a Highland saying: '1746 was the year when little wheels and red soldiers were introduced'.) A double driving band (in reality one continuous length of twine) passes around the wheel's rim, with one band around the spindle end and the other passing over a whorl connected to a bobbin. This wheel, therefore, performs the two spinning tasks, twisting the fibres and winding the spun yarn on to a bobbin simultaneously, with the added advantage of requring the spinner to sit down when working, as the wheel was turned by means of a foot treadle.

While the simple muckle-wheel could be made at home, the more complicated flyer wheels were made by specialist craftsmen, who would often decorate the 'stock' with notchings, and turned the spokes and legs elaborately. It is traditional for wheels made in Scotland to have the name of the maker, and the place of origin, carved into the stock.

There is a story of Highland spinners removing the driving band of their wheel at night 'so that the fairies can do no spinning'. This could, however, have been a way of avoiding possible damage from the wheel being turned by the children of the household.

THE GREAT, OR MUCKLE, WHEEL

TH'US YIN
THU'S NO YIN
AN' THU'S YIN A OOT

THU'S TWA
THU'S NO TWO
AN' THU'S TWA A OOT

A Dumfries-shire verse recited when winding yarn on to a hand reel

THE FLYER, OR SAXONY, WHEEL

DYES AND DYEING

Although the very earliest check cloths woven in the Highlands were probably made from the natural black, grey and white of the sheep's fleece, the desire for colour and variety soon demanded the use of dyes to colour the wool fibres. There is little information about early Highland dye recipes, and it is difficult to understand how some of the complicated dye processes were discovered: most of the plants used for vegetable dyeing give no external clue of the colours which they will yield, and only a few are 'substantive' (give off their dye simply, in boiling water). Most are 'adjective', and need processing with chemicals before they produce colour on fibres. Certainly the lichen (a curious symbiotic relationship between a fungus and an algae) has always been in abundant supply in the Highland region, and its many varieties are capable of producing a whole spectrum of colours. There was even an attempt to use them on a commercial scale in Glasgow in the late 18th and early 19th centuries, but they were eclipsed by a superior imported species. Chemical dyestuffs were discovered in the middle of the 19th century, and from that time hardly any natural dyes were used by industry.

Vegetable dyeing is not without its risks; for example, dyes obtained from the same species of plant will vary from one area to the next. All sorts of conditions will affect the colours obtained: the soil in which the plant grew; the local climate; the geology, affecting the minerals in the water. The time of year in which the dye plant was gathered, and the way in which it was stored until use, can alter the dye colours. The nature of the wool being dyed is yet another factor: the hard fine wool of the Highland sheep would not take dye readily, and the fibres had to be steeped in the dye liquor for days or even weeks to obtain a strong fast colour. (Wool from Lowland sheep was softer, and often woollen spun, as opposed to the worsted spinning of the Highland yarn, so it absorbed dye more readily.) The vessel in which the dyeing was done played an important part – an iron pot would dull the colours substantially.

Vegetable dyeing played a large part in the evolution of tartan setts. Where a particular dye plant was prolific in the neighbourhood of a tartan weaver, that colour would predominate in the tartan of that area, and of the local clan. The yarn was dyed in small quantities, because of the size of the vessels, and successive dye batches, even with the same recipes, would vary in colour. Tartans with narrow bands of colour in the warp would be popular, as any change in colour would be much less obvious in such a sett. It

Wool dyed with natural dyes.

is interesting to note that many very early tartan cloths show no repeat of pattern in warp or weft, indicating that the stripe proportions were often dependent on the amount of yarn in any one batch of colour.

PREPARATION OF THE WOOL FOR DYEING

There are three stages at which colour, in the form of dye, can be applied to fibres. The loose fibres can be dyed *before* spinning, which enables them to be blended together: for example, some red fibres mixed with some blue ones would produce a purple yarn when spun. (Weavers favour the subtle blends obtainable by this method, hence the origin of the compliment 'dyed-in-the-wool' which indicates soundness of character.) Alternatively, the yarn can be spun straight from the fleece, subsequently to be dyed 'in the yarn' and when dyeing for tartan weaving it has always been more usual for this second process to be used. The third stage at which dye can be applied is when the cloth has actually been woven, but this is not, of course, applicable to tartan.

Before dyeing by any method, the natural grease (or lanolin) must be removed from the fleece, and for spinning fine yarns it is better to do this when the fleece is in its unspun state. It is washed in soft water (bran can be used to soften the water at this stage), and steeped in an alkaline solution. In early days, stale human urine was frequently used for this process; later, soda ash made from burnt seaweed (or kelp) was a useful alternative. The wool is then dried, and 'teased out' to remove any extraneous matter or lumps.

A little light oil is re-introduced in the wool to provide lubrication which enables the individual fibres to slip past one another and form a lump-free yarn. After spinning, the yarn is washed to remove the oil so that it is ready to receive the dye.

MORDANTS

The word 'mordant' comes from the French 'mordre', to bite. Mordants are metallic salts which are applied to the wool fibres, in fleece or yarn form, which will help certain dyestuffs to combine with (or 'bite' into) the fibres. Weavers in the Highlands would use alum, iron and copper as mordants for 'adjective' dyes. These would be applied to the wool before dyeing, and sometimes another mordant would be added after dyeing, to alter the colour. Some of these mordants would have been imported into Scotland – there are records of alum being brought into Leith in 1491. In the late 16th century, alum mining began in several parts of Britain, including Scotland. Iron mordant could be obtained from certain black bogs in Scotland. Some plants could act as mordants: the fir-club moss could take the place of alum. It was also known that oak-galls could darken or dull a colour. Most lichens, one of the most common sources of dye in the Highlands, needed no mordants.

COLOURS OBTAINED FROM DYE PLANTS

REDS AND PURPLES

These colours would have been obtained from orchil, which is produced by some lichens. This was known in Scotland as cudbear (Gaelic: *corcar* or *corcur*), and was made mainly from the lichens *Ochrolechia tartarea* and *Urceolaria calcarea*. These lichens have to be soaked in ammonia (stale urine would have been used) before they release first the red, then the purple dyestuff. (Other lichens are substantive: they give a dye in boiling water.) Crotal (or crottle), is the Highland name given to lichens used for dyeing, and various lichens are known as Black, Dark, White or Light Crotal. *Ochrolechia tartarea* would be gathered during May and June, usually in days following rain, as all lichens are easier to find and to pick in these conditions. In dry weather they are almost invisible, and are brittle to pick. Lichens are very slow-growing, taking years to reach maturity, and this one must be at least five years old before it is gathered as a dye plant. It was steeped in putrid human urine for three to four weeks, and kept gently warm during the process. (As in most parts of the world, human urine was used in Scotland for several processes during the dyeing of fibres. It was known genteelly as the 'home solution' by Scottish weavers, and called 'fual' or 'graith'. An easily available source of alkali (or ammonia), it was collected by dyers from neighbouring households, with male urine being favoured over female. Animal urine could be used, but richer colours were obtained by using the human variety. The term 'spending a penny' arose from the practice of selling urine to dyers and other users of this ubiquitous product.) When fermented, the paste of lichen and urine could be stored for future use by forming it into balls, wrapping it in dock leaves and hanging it in the smoke of the peat fire. It could then be powdered into boiling water and used when needed.

The lichens *Parmelia omphalodes* and *Parmelia saxatilis* were both used extensively also, as they were known to be very fast dyes, to produce reds varying from red/brown to red/purple. It was believed that stockings dyed in this way would protect the wearer from blisters on long walks. *Ochrolechia parella* was used when a reddish-orange dye was needed. When used with ammonia a soft claret red can be obtained.

Red dye could also have been obtained from ladies' bedstraw *(Gallium verum)*, which is a member of the madder family *(Rubiaceae)*. The Gaelic word for red is *ruadh,* and is especially identified with this plant, which gives dye from its roots. The roots of tormentil *(Potentilla erecta)* were known to have been used in the Orkneys to dye wool reddish-purple with an alum mordant. In the 17th century, dyer's madder *(Rubia tinctoria),* was imported into Scotland, and would then have been used to supplement native dye plants.

Other reds and purples can be obtained from:
Bramble *(Rubus fruticosus* agg)
Spindle *(Euonymus europaeus)*
Dandelion roots *(Taraxacum officinale* agg)
Sundew *(Drosera rotundifolia)* – (used with ammonia and copperas)
St John's wort *(Hypericum perforatum)* – (the yellow flowerheads give purple-red when used without a mordant)

Purple yarn could, of course, be obtained by overdyeing a red with a blue dye, and *vice versa,* or by blending together red and blue dyed fleece before spinning.

YELLOWS AND BROWNS

A lichen called dark crotal *(Hypogymnia physodes)* was used extensively for golden-brown dye, which it gives off in boiling water. The stone crotal *(Parmelia caperata)* produces a good yellow on wool, again in boiling water. One which grows in Scotland only on trees – *Platysma glaucum* – gives a yellow to wool with boiling water also. These dyes, needing no mordant, would often be used with indigo, to give greens. Many other lichens would also have been used. Other plants which gave yellow were: heather, bracken roots, birch leaves, broom flowers, bog myrtle, St John's wort (with alum mordant), onion skins, and the bark, shoots and flowers of the gorse bush (known in Scotland as 'whin').

Most brown dyes came from lichens or tree bark. Those like oak contain tannin, producing brown dye when mordanted with alum, and black when mordanted with iron. The husks and roots of the walnut tree, and the roots of water-lilies, give good browns, as do dulse (seaweed), larch needles, pine cones, and juniper berries.

BLUES

Blue dye can be obtained from the lichen *Xanthoria parientina,* when the wool has been steeped for a long time and then exposed to bright sunlight (see *Lichens for Vegetable Dyeing* by Eileen Bolton, published by Studio Vista in the UK and Robin & Russ Handweavers, Oregon, USA).

The leaves of devil's bit scabious *(Scabiosa succisa)* are known to produce a good blue, and this plant was prolific in the Highlands. The Gaelic word for blue is *glas,* derived from the Latin for woad, *glastum,* and a list of Highland dye plants in 1883 mentions woad, but it is not known to be native to Scotland, and was probably imported from Holland. In the 13th century, Scotland was recorded as trading with the Low Countries, often exchanging cloth for dyestuffs. Woad was probably replaced by the much stronger blue dyestuff, indigo, in the 18th century. Even today, some commercial dyers use this vegetable dye as it is probably the only colour which cannot be copied successfully by chemical means. It is obtained from the leaf of plants of the genus *Indigofera.* There are records of regular shipments of indigo from Holland to St Kilda in 1700, and in 1810 the staggering amount of three million pounds of indigo was imported to Britain from India. Indigo imparts a powerful blue, and can be used for overdyeing, so that yellow yarn dyed in indigo becomes a vibrant green and red yarn becomes a strong purple. Indigo arrived in hard balls of paste, which had to be ground into a powder. It is insoluble in water, and has to be fermented (again, stale urine was used). After steeping in the solution, the wool would be removed from the dye bath and would then turn blue on being exposed to air: the dyestuff contained in the plant, and appearing as a yellowish colour, absorbs oxygen from the air and changes colour

GATHERING CROTAL, 1939, ISLE OF HARRIS.

dramatically. Further immersion and oxidization will produce deeper colours.

Other sources of blue dye were the whortleberry, blaeberry, or bilberry *(Vaccinum myrtillus)*, elderberry *(Sambucas nigra)*, and the root of the yellow iris *(Iris pseudacorus)*.

GREENS

A green yarn would often have been obtained by over-dyeing: a yellow yarn might have been dipped briefly — in indigo, for instance, to produce a rich emerald. But some dye plants obtainable in the Highlands give softer greens and these include elder, mares' tails *(Equisetum)*, nettles, reeds, sorrel, ling *(Calluna Vulgaris)* and bracken shoots.

BLACK

Black was obtained by using the bark of the alder tree *(Alnus glutinosus)*, mordanted with iron. This would sometimes be used on yarn which was spun from the fleece of 'black' sheep (producing a very dark brown wool which needed little dye to make it black).

The root of the yellow iris will produce black on wool which has been mordanted with alum, and the roots of meadow sweet *(Spirea ulmaria)* were also used in the Highlands as a black dye.

Walnut shells and husks were sometimes used in combination with woad to give black, but only on coarse wool as it produced a hard handle.

FASHIONS IN TARTAN COLOURING

Although the actual hue of the tartan sett often remains unchanged through the years, the tone and intensity of the colour will often be varied, by demand or by commercial endeavour. In Victorian times, for instance, it was fashionable for the colours to be very dark, and the blues and greens of some tartans became almost black. Recognition of the different setts could be quite difficult, and when these Victorian cloths appeared in portraits painted in oils the subsequent darkening of the varnish only added to the confusion. About 1914, there was a revival of so-called 'ancient' colours — chemically dyed to match the earlier natural dyes. These softer colourings are still popular, and are sometimes known as 'old colours', or O.C. Around 1945, 'reproduction' or 'muted' colours were introduced which simulated the faded and worn qualities of the early vegetable-dyed cloths. Black was often included — erroneously. (Wool dyed black by natural means or used directly from a black sheep would usually have faded to a yellow/brown.) The clearer 'modern' colouring is now often thought to be the more authentic.

Hunting setts should not be confused with the 'ancient' or 'reproduction' colourings. They evolved through the need to wear a less conspicuous tartan while out hunting on the hillsides, and often substitute greens and browns for the brighter blues and reds of the standard clan or family tartan.

Confusion can arise sometimes when a sett (the term for the arrangement and proportion of colours in a particular tartan) is called 'ancient sett'. This does not refer to the actual colours, but to the antiquity of the proportional design, and an 'ancient sett' can be made in modern colours.

When white yarns are used as part of a multi-coloured cloth, they will, after several washings, take on a light colouring as the dye from adjacent stripes bleeds into them. This could account for a few interesting 'alterations' to original setts. In the study of old tartans, the existence of white is often an assumption: the light yarns can be very light blues, greys yellows etc. In Macalister, for instance, the light green (which is not found in many other tartans) is, in all cases, found next to a dark green stripe, and was almost certainly caused by bleeding dye.

TOP; MUTED FRASER, CENTRE; ANCIENT FRASER, BOTTOM; MODERN FRASER.

HANDWEAVING A TARTAN CLOTH TODAY

Tartans appear to be simple cloths — their 2 × 2 weave is familiar to weavers and needs only four shafts (harnesses) – but to weave a perfect tartan is one of the most demanding tasks which a handweaver can undertake: it requires excellent craftsmanship in warping, dressing the loom and in weaving. The planning of the cloth must, as usual, take into account its end use. The choice of fibre and yarn will depend on this, as will the sett of the yarn. The tartan sett chosen must be placed so that emphatic stripes occur in suitable places, again according to the end use. A complete number of repeats will be necessary, if the cloth is to be joined edge to edge or cut economically.

Whatever the fibre, and the yarn used, some rules apply to the successful weaving of a tartan cloth:

1. The yarn used must be of the same material in both warp and weft.
2. The balance of the warp and weft must be equal (i.e. the same number of ends and picks per inch) so that the colours in the check design are seen equally in warp and weft. The sett should be very carefully calculated (remembering that the ends can be sett more closely for 2 × 2 twill than for plain weaves).
3. The weave should normally be 2 × 2 twill (see page 30).
4. The weaving should be even, so that the diagonal line of the twill is exactly 45 degrees across the cloth, and consistently so for the length of the woven piece. Any wavering of this diagonal will be due either to uneven tension in the warp or to uneven beating of the weft (even a short pause can affect the beat). Because the cloth is balanced, equal numbers of a colour in warp and weft must produce a perfect square where they cross. This essential feature provides a useful clue system for the colour order of the weft: as it is exactly the same as in the warp, the best way to make sure that the weft stripes are correctly inserted is to trace a diagonal line of self-colour crossings in perfect squares from the left selvedge. If the area formed by the crossing of the same number of weft and warp threads is anything other than square, adjust the beating to correct the fault. Do not be tempted to weave more or fewer weft threads in order to produce a perfect square, as this will affect the way in which the cloth behaves. If a complete number of repeats is being woven, when the diagonal of squares reaches the opposite selvedge it can be started again from the left hand side, and so on until the warp is finished.

WARPING

The warping of a tartan must, of course, be planned and executed accurately. Depending on the tartan being woven and the yarn used, a certain number of repeats of the sett will be possible across the cloth, varying from many repeats of the MacGregor Rob Roy to perhaps only one of the complicated Ogilvie of Airlie. Because of the many ways of warping and dressing a loom, it is impossible to give full instructions which will apply to all weavers, but it is generally agreed that sectional warping is almost always impossible, unless the tartan chosen and the 'sett' of the yarn coincide to produce a repeat of exactly 2 or 4 inches. Because of the many colours involved in most tartan warps, it is usually easier to warp on to pegs on a frame or board rather than on a mill, so that the colours can be held at one end without breaking off for each strip. (This is the obvious explanation for the fact that, to this day, warping mills are not generally used by Scottish weavers, even

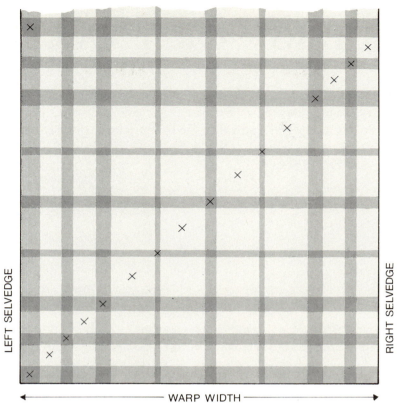

A TARTAN CLOTH, AS IT WOULD APPEAR ON THE LOOM, WITH THE 'REFERENCE' SQUARES INDICATED WITH CROSSES (SEE RULE 4, ON OPPOSITE PAGE).

in Colleges of Art. Pegged warping frames are universally used.) Those weavers who prefer to thread their looms from front to back, have an alternative method available to them: separate warps are made of each colour (all the warp ends of that colour in the number of repeats required in the warp) and chained. The colours can then be distributed in the reed before entering and beaming. The main colour should be distributed first, followed by the secondary colour, and so on. This method of entering is usually only suitable for comparatively short warps, and in cases where the warp ends are sleyed singly, or in pairs, in the reed.

SELVEDGES

The planning of the selvedges depends, as always, on the purpose of the cloth to be woven. Some weavers prefer to thread the first and last four ends 1, 3, 2, 4 for extra strength. No extra threads should be necessary, especially if, as good weaving practice demands, the selvedges are never touched with the fingers or shuttle during weaving. Some weavers, however, prefer to double up the first and last pairs of ends. Depending on the tartan being woven, decisions on breaking and restarting a weft colour must also take into account the end use of the cloth, as well as the distance involved. If the selvedges are not to be seen then it is better to carry the colours up the side of the cloth, ready for the next insertion, except in the case of very long floats. This will not only save time, but also prevent a thickening of the selvedge, with resultant unsatisfactory build up of the fabric edge on the cloth beam. Because stripes in tartan are always of an even number of threads, all will begin and end on the same selvedge.

When weaving a tartan, it is not good practice to overlap new and old wefts of the same colour midway across the warp, as this will give a slight thickness of colour which will spoil the even nature of the design.

THE DESIGN OF A TARTAN

Basically, all tartans are formed by an arrangement of coloured stripes in the warp (the lengthwise threads in a length of cloth) with the same arrangement of coloured stripes in the weft (the threads across the width of the cloth).

WARP STRIPES

WEFT STRIPES

When these two sets of threads are interwoven at right angles to one another, the result is a tartan.

Except for some very early examples, the checks of the tartan repeat themselves across the cloth (the size of the repeat depending on the tartan sett involved, and the thickness of the thread being woven). Most tartans repeat in what is called a 'mirror' repeat, in which one half of the design is an exact reverse of the other.

Fraser of Lovat

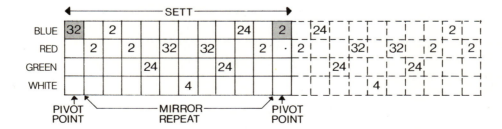

The points where the repeat starts to reverse is called the 'pivot' of the design.

Although tartans were certainly never conceived within the framework of a system of designing, it is interesting for anyone studying the subject to be able to identify some of the design elements in tartan development.

48

The simplest of all tartans is the equal width striping in warp and weft, of two colours. Examples of this are the MacGregor Rob Roy in red and black, and the Moncreiffe in red and green.

MacGregor Rob Roy

The next simple variation on this is to add an *overcheck* (a thin line of colour in warp and weft) often simply reversing the colour, on the centre of each band of colour. Sometimes a double-line overcheck is used, as in Erskine.

Erskine

The next elaboration is where the broad warp and weft bands are broken up into several smaller bands, each separated by a thin line of the other main colour e.g. MacMillan, MacQuarrie. An overcheck is sometimes added to this e.g. Hamilton.

MacQuarrie  Hamilton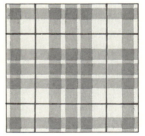

Sometimes the edges of the bands, in warp and weft, are 'broken' (e.g. Menzies) or have another colour added (MacDonnell of Keppoch).

MacDonnell of Keppoch

Setts then increase in complexity in many ways, from the multicolour, varied-width striping on a plain ground, as in the Royal and Dress Stewarts, and Macbeth, to the complications of the Ogilvie of Airlie, and the few asymmetric tartans such as the Buchanan.

THE WEAVERS OF KILBARCHAN

This evocative description of the hand-weaving of tartan cloth is taken from *In Scotland Again* by H. V. Morton, published by Methuen in 1933.

When I was approaching Paisley I remembered a promise made long ago to a ripe and knowledgeable Scotman:

'If ever you are near Paisley,' he said, 'get away from it quickly and go to Kilbarchan. Although it is only a few miles from Glasgow no one knows about it, and it is one of the most interesting places in the country. Promise to go there.'

So I turned off at Johnstone and came in time to a place where the Paisley tramcars end. There was a long, steepish hill and on the top of it was the village of Kilbarchan, the last place left in Scotland where a colony of hand-loom weavers make clan tartans.

I gave one glance at streets which climb and descend hills flanked on each side by solid-stone whitewashed houses whose front doors are flush with the road, and I knew that something from the eighteenth century had managed to survive the twentieth. Kilbarchan is an astonishing place. The deliberate ending of the tramcar at the foot of its hill is pleasingly symbolic. Everything that has made Glasgow, Paisley, and all the satellite towns of Lanarkshire, stops short at Kilbarchan's hill. Here is a little lowland town with its feet in the eighteenth century. Its survival is all the more remarkable because it stands in the heart of one of the largest industrial centres in Great Britain. How Kilbarchan has resisted the cheap allurements of this age I really do not know.

I looked through a window which, like most of the windows in Kilbarchan, was low and flush with the street. Inside sat an old woman at a hand loom. I heard the clack-clack of the flying shuttle. The evening sun fell through the window and lit up a piece of red dress tartan which the woman was making. I watched her for a long time. She would consult a ticket which hung on the loom in front of her, change a shuttle loaded with red wool for one loaded with green, and then — clack-clack, clack-clack, clack-clack — and a thin green line would grow on the edge of the red cloth.

I entered and talked to her. She looked at me over the rim of her spectacles and went on making the tartan, answering me as she worked. She told me that in Kilbarchan is the last colony of hand-loom tartan weavers in Scotland. Each one is over fifty years of age, most of them are women and one old man is over eighty.

'And when we're deid', she said, 'there'll be nane to come efter us, for the young ones wilna learn the loom!'

Fifty years ago, she told me, there were eight hundred looms working in Kilbarchan, making clan tartans as fast as they could. To-day there are only twenty looms and no apprentices to follow on, because the young girl and the young man of to-day want more money and don't like hard work.

I sought out Mr. John Borland, who knows all about the tartan weavers of Kilbarchan. He is nearly seventy, but has the bright blue eyes of a man of thirty. He was wearing a tweed jacket, with the red-piped trousers and waistcoat of a postman. Yes, it was true! The hand-made tartan would end with the twenty weavers. There were still 'big bugs' — Hielanmen — who insisted that their kilts should be made by hand, as the tartan was made for their forefathers. And they would not wear chemically dyed tartan either. It had to be vegetable dye, as it was in the old days, and it had to be woven by hand as it was in old times, tough, hand-woven tartan that would never wear out.

So said John Borland.

My visit to the last twenty tartan weavers of Kilbarchan was one of the most delightful experiences I have had in Scotland.

I would enter a small house. Looms filled the front rooms. Although it was dusk the shuttles were clacking like mad, for, as one old lady put it, 'nae weaver wastes daylight'. In some a white-haired woman — for most of the weavers are women between fifty and seventy — sat at a spinning wheel and handed the wool straight from the wheel to her companion at the loom.

The good nature, the good humour, the easy courtesy, the simplicity, and the lovableness of these old people went to my heart. They knew nothing except that they were weaving tartan for a cloth merchant. He would send down the material and the instructions for the sett. They simply had to follow out the regulation pattern: so many threads of red, so many green, then so many white, and so on. A quick worker could make from seven to ten yards in a day. Miss Bella

Borland, one of the quickest, can do ten. The pay per yard is 11½d. or 1s.

This seemed miserably inadequate to my mind, when hand-made tartan is probably 15s. or 20s. a yard, possibly more, but the weavers refused to feel under-paid.

'It's the best Botany wool,' they explained, 'and it's verra expensive. We havena ony responsibility but to weave it. . . .'

They took pride in bringing for my inspection fine lengths of tartan — Munro, MacKenzie, MacLean of Duart, the gaudy yellow Buchanan, and that most difficult of all tartans to weave, the Ogilvie.

I met 'Sandy' Grey, who is over eighty years of age. He started weaving tartan seventy years ago. He stood in Shuttle Street (what a name!), and told me how Kilbarchan sounded in his youth when eight hundred looms were working from daylight to dark.

I also met the 'baby' of Kilbarchan, William Meikle, who is fifty! In a few years' time loom after loom will become silent and a great and historic industry will be dead.

'Aye, it's a tragedy,' said William Meikle, 'for there's no other trade like weaving where a man can make his ain money in his ain hame and sit at the loom watching the flowers in his garden. . . .'

The strange thing about William Meikle is that he has learnt this difficult art of tartan weaving since the war. When he came out of the army — he served with the Argyll and Sutherland Highlanders — he decided to go back to the trade of his fathers. To-day he is the only man in Scotland — probably in the world — who can weave two clan tartans at once.

These are travelling rugs.

On one side is the husband's tartan, on the other the wife's. I watched him at work on a rug of Grant tartan, the reverse side of which was a MacLean. It was an extraordinarily complicated process.

'How on earth do you do it?' I asked.

'Well, my eye's on the MacLean and my mind's on the Grant.'

This is probably the most difficult hand-loom job a man could tackle.

WEAVER'S COTTAGE, KILBARCHAN

THE TARTANS

THE NAME
When looking up a tartan, the name of the clan or family under which the tartan is shown may not be exactly the same as the one which is sought. It must be remembered that often, even in living memory, the spelling of a surname will have changed subtly, and certainly it is likely to do so over centuries and across continents. For example, the name Eliot can be spelt in many ways, as this verse from the annals of a Border Club shows:

> ELLIOT, ELIOTT, ELIOT, ELLIOTT
>
> The double L and single T
> Descend from Minto and Wolflee;
> The double T and single L
> Mark the old race in Stobs that dwell;
> The single L and single T
> The Eliots of St Germains be;
> But double T and double L
> Who they are, nobody can tell.

It must also be remembered that the prefix 'Mac' means 'son of', so by adding 'Mac' to the beginning of a name, the family tartan may be discovered. Similarly, if the surname already ends in 'son', then by removing that, and adding 'Mac' to the beginning of the name, the Scottish equivalent may be found. As an extreme example of this, the name Thomson is the anglicized version of the Scottish name MacTavish.

THE HISTORY
The history of individual tartans has been recorded sketchily, if at all, in the past. Often there is nothing known about the origin of a cloth, as it was almost certainly originally regarded as an unimportant necessity, and not worthy of special records. The only positive record, in many cases, is in the list of the early commercial weavers, and where this occurs it has been noted. The fact, however, that a tartan is mentioned as having been 'first recorded in the lists of Wilsons of Bannockburn in 1819' is no indication that this is the date of its origin, merely that it certainly predates that time. Conversely, where a tartan is listed as having been 'first recorded in the *Vestiarium Scoticum*', this is an indication that it might not have been in existence before the compilation of that imaginative publication by the Sobieski brothers. (See page 25.) A note that 'this is a modern tartan' should not be regarded as anything other than that this tartan is part of the living, growing interest in clan and family tartans, and has been evolved to fill the need for a tartan in the life of the family today. The term 'modern' can often mean fifty years old.

THE PHOTOGRAPHS
Some of the tartans photographed have been woven in modern colours, and others in ancient colours (these are marked A. C. in the caption). (See page 45.)

Wherever possible, the samples show as much as possible of one repeat of the sett, but sometimes the size of the repeat makes this impracticable. Sometimes it will be apparent that the tartan photographed differs from the thread count given. This is not necessarily a mistake, but shows an alternative sett. Often eight or ten variations have been recorded: too many and too confusing to include in a book of this type. In all cases the chosen thread counts and illustrations have been recommended as being the most authentic on record. All the tartan cloths appear on the page in their actual size and it is often possible to 'read' an alternative thread count directly from the photograph.

READING THE THREAD COUNTS

The 'sett' of a tartan refers to the complete pattern of stripes in both warp and weft. The 'thread count' is the indication to weavers of the warp colour arrangement and proportion. (This is almost always identical to that of the weft.) It is important to realize that the numbers shown are not, necessarily, the actual numbers of threads in the stripes, but the *lowest* numbers possible and that they represent a proportion guide. When using finer threads it will often be necessary to double or treble these numbers to obtain a sett of the desired size. There is no 'preferred size' of sett for a tartan: the scale of the pattern is planned in relation to the end use. When woven for a kilt, for example, a large-scale sett is common. Material for a tie will need the smallest sett possible in that tartan, and 'miniaturization' of tartans, sometimes by reducing large background colour areas, is common for that purpose.

In most books on tartan the thread counts are usually shown as a line of letters and numbers eg W2, Bk4, R16 etc. Although this is an adequate way in which to record the sett of a tartan, the grid system used in this book has been evolved so that weavers can 'see' the rhythm of a sett, and are able to assess at a glance the numbers of colours, and the approximate quantity of each colour yarn which will be needed.

When reading any tartan thread count, the following points must be understood:

1. Only half a full repeat is shown: the full repeat is completed by 'mirror imaging' the half repeat. This can be illustrated by actually standing a small mirror on the pivot point at either end of the chart.
2. Pivot points are indicated, where used, at both ends of the thread count, by the number appearing on a shaded square. This indicates that, when repeating the count in mirror image, the pivot point is used actually as a pivot and is not repeated. Occasionally the sett is an asymmetric one (indicated by a warning note in each case), and repeats in a simple straight sequence, not in mirror image. No pivot points are therefore necessary.
3. Sometimes a stripe will be described as white/yellow. This means that these two colours alternate throughout the cloth in that stripe position – white in the first half of the sett, yellow in the mirror image.

HOW TO READ THE DIAGRAMS OF THE SETTS

The tartan setts in the following pages have been presented in a way which will, at first, seem curious to readers of other books on tartans, but which will be familiar to weavers. It is hoped that this method will present the proportions and placing of the various stripes in visibly recognizable sequence. It should be possible to see in this diagrammatic form the predominance of a background colour, and the rhythms of the striping. Most setts have a 'pivot point' at each end. This has been denoted by a shaded background to the number, and this marked stripe **is not repeated** in the **mirror** repeat which should follow. (See page 48.) The setts should be read from one pivot point to the other, and then back across to the first, and so on. Note that a few tartans are asymmetrical, and repeat simply from left to right so that no pivot point is marked.

The numbers alongside the colours do not necessarily represent threads, but the proportion of the coloured band. The sett can be woven with units of threads of these numbers, if the thread being used and the size of the repeat required coincide with these. They can all be doubled, trebled, etc. to produce the size of repeat needed. The minimum number used is two, because it is usually impracticable to weave single weft threads of a colour. In the sett for the simple MacGregor (Rob Roy) it will be seen that each band is marked as '2', although it would clearly not be a tartan at all if only two threads were used. However, as the relative proportion of the bands is equal, the correct number is the minimum of two, to be multiplied as the thread and repeat size demands.

ABERCROMBIE

This sett was Pattern No. 64 or 'Abercrombie' in the Wilson Key Pattern Book (1819). It is now known at Graham of Montrose (see page 79).

GREEN	28	14				
WHITE		2				
BLACK			14	4	4	
BLUE				4	4	28

ALLISON

This tartan was first recorded in John Ross's list in 1930.

MID BLUE	6	30					
BLACK	6	30			30		6
YELLOW			6				2
GREEN				30	30		
BLUE				6			
WHITE						6	
ROYAL BLUE						8	
RED							12

BLUE	6	24					
BLACK	6		36	4	16	16	4
GREEN				28	28		
YELLOW					4		
LT. BLUE						8	
RED						8	
WHITE							6

ANDERSON (MACANDREW)

A tartan probably dating from the first quarter of the 19th century, and with the rare feature of a light blue ground, sometimes appearing as grey, or turquoise.

RED	6	2		2				2	6	4	8
LT. BLUE		12			36						
BLACK			4			6	6	2	8	8	
WHITE						6					
YELLOW								2	2		
GREEN										12	12

ANGUS

First recorded and illustrated in Johnson's book of 1906. It is thought to have originally been designed for a family, as in the case of Nairn. Now used in a form of district sett for Angus.

BLACK	6	64				
RED		2		2	2	6
BLUE			56	4	4	

ARBUTHNOT

A modern family tartan, one of the few to be recorded by the Lyon Court.

BLUE	8	2	2			4				10	2
BLACK		2	2	8					8	2	
GREEN					4	4	4	4			
WHITE						2		2			

ARMSTRONG
The Armstrongs are a Lowland family, and as such probably had no tartan until this sett appeared in *Vestiarium Scoticum* in 1842.

GREEN	4	60				
BLACK		2	24	2	2	
BLUE				4	2	24
RED						6

BAILEY, BAILLIE
The thread count shown is of Bailey of Polkemett. There is an older sett, worn by the Bailey Fencibles (Territorial Army).

GREEN	4			
RED	40			
BLACK		24		
BLUE			24	
WHITE				6

BAIRD
This sett was first recorded in 1906.

PURPLE	6	2			
GREEN		2	16		
BLACK			16	4	
BLUE				16	6

BARCLAY, dress, BARCLAY, hunting
The Barclays originate from Aberdeenshire, and would have had no tartan before the publication of *Vestiarium Scoticum* in 1842, where the sett for the hunting version (b) made its first appearance. The Barclay dress (a) sett is of more recent date.

a)

WHITE	2		
YELLOW		12	2
BLACK		12	

b)

RED	2		
GREEN		32	2
BLUE		32	

BIRRELL or BIRRAL
First recorded in Wilson of Bannockburn's list of 1819.

PURPLE	16		4				8		8		
WHITE		4			4	4		4		4	
RED		8		8							64
ROSE			4	4							
GREEN							32				
LT. BLUE								4	4		

BLAIR
A 20th-century tartan, based on a simplified MacDonald.

BLUE	12	40			
RED		4		4	
BLACK			32		
GREEN				40	12

BORTHWICK

DK. RED	8				20	
BLACK		4	28	4		2
GREY			20		20	
GREEN						24

BORTHWICK, dress

First recorded in 1951, this tartan was made for the family of Borthwick of Crookston.

BLACK	4		28	4		2
WHITE		20		20		
DK. RED					20	
GREEN						24

BOYD

This tartan was designed for the Earl of Kilmarnock in 1948. It was based on the Black Watch tartan.

YELLOW	10							
GREEN		44				10		
BLACK			4	4	20			8
BLUE			4	4				
RED						76	8	
WHITE								10

BRODIE, dress, BRODIE, hunting

The Brodie dress sett (c) is alleged to have appeared first in a mid-18th century portrait. It also appeared in *Vestiarium Scoticum* (1842), but a different sett was in use about 1850, as is given here (b). The hunting sett is of more recent origin.

a)
BLACK	4	16		16
RED		32		4
YELLOW			2	

b)
RED	96			24	2
WHITE		8			
BLUE			8		8
BLACK			8		
YELLOW					8

c)
RED	4				4
BLUE		16			
GREEN			16		
BLACK				16	16
YELLOW				2	

BRUCE

This sett appeared in *Vestiarium Scoticum,* and was claimed to be of ancient origin. In the late 18th century two other designs were in commercial production: 'Bruce' (now the MacColl sett) and 'New Bruce' (now Grant).

WHITE/YELLOW	2			
RED		16	4	2
GREEN			4	12

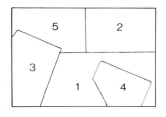

Photographs on pages 56 & 57
1. Abercrombie A.C.
2. Anderson
3. Angus A.C.
4. Armstrong
5. Blair

BRUCE OF KINNAIRD

This is a variation on the tartan 'Prince Charles Edward'. Lord Elgin, Chief of the Bruces, has a coat in his possession worn by James Bruce of Kinnaird who was the 18th-century explorer. It has been used by Lord Elgin's family as a dress tartan since the 1950s.

RED	56						
GREEN		50					
BLACK			4	4	34		
WHITE				14			4
YELLOW					4		
LT. BLUE						12	
ROSE							14

BUCHAN

A family tartan, derived from Cumming, to whom the Buchans are related.

BLACK	4			12			48		4
RED		4	4		12	4		4	
GREEN			54			12			
BLUE					4				4

N.B. Double pivot band

BUCHANAN

The asymmetric Buchanan sett (a) is one of the most popular tartans today; its attractive and unusual irregularity could have been due to a mistake made in copying down the sett from a drawing of 1845 by MacIain (who was not noted for his accuracy). Sett (b) is thought to be more authentic. Sett (c) was recorded in *Vestiarium Scoticum*.

a)
BLACK	2		2		2		2	2		2	2	
YELLOW		12										12
BLUE				8		8		8			8	
GREEN					12	12						
RED							16		16			
WHITE										2		

N.B. This sett is asymmetric.

b)
LT. BLUE	4		4				4	
GREEN		32						
BLACK				2	2	2	2	2
YELLOW					8	8		
RED								32
WHITE								4

c)
BLACK	2			
WHITE		18	4	4
DK. RED			8	8

BUCHANAN, hunting

This sett was recorded in the Highland Society of London, at a later date than the rest of the Collection there.

LT. BLUE	2		12			12			12		
GREEN		24									24
BLACK			4	4	4	4	4		4	4	
BUFF				24	24						
MAROON							24	24			
WHITE								2			

N.B. This sett is asymmetric.

BURNETT

RED	120	10	10	10	
BLUE		10			
WHITE			4		
GREEN				4	
YELLOW					4

59

CAMERON, clan
This clan tartan was first illustrated in the *Vestiarium Scoticum*.

YELLOW	2			
RED		30	2	2
GREEN			12	12

CAMERON, hunting
This sett, based on one in the *Vestiarium Scoticum*, was adopted at a Clan Gathering in 1956.

RED	6		6			
GREEN		20		28	6	
BLUE					32	
YELLOW						4

CAMERON OF LOCHIEL

RED	12		12			4		8
GREEN			6					
BLUE					2		2	16
WHITE					2			

CAMPBELL OF ARGYLL, or CAMPBELL OF LOCHAWE

BLUE	2		16					2		2		16
BLACK		2		16		2		2	16		2		2
GREEN					16				16				
WHITE/YELLOW						4						

CAMPBELL OF BREADALBANE
Sett (a) was worn by the Fencibles of Breadalbane from their embodiment in 1793 to their disbandment in 1802. Sett (b) the 'fancy' Breadalbane appeared, based on 'Abercrombie', Pattern No. 64 in the Wilson Key Pattern Book of 1819.

a)
BLUE	2		16				2	2		16
BLACK		2		16			16	2	2	
YELLOW					2	2				
GREEN						28				

b)
BLACK	6		18			18
BLUE		18				
GREEN				18	18	
YELLOW					4	

CAMPBELL OF CAWDOR
This sett is otherwise known as Macorqudale.

LT. BLUE	4				
BLACK		2	16	2	
GREEN		16			
BLUE				16	
RED					4

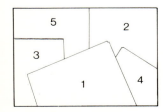

Photographs on pages 60 & 61
1. Brodie (dress)
2. Bruce
3. Bruce of Kinnaird
4. Buchanan (special colours)
5. Burnett of Leys A.C.

CARMICHAEL

BLACK	6			
GREEN		72		
BLUE			56	4
RED				4
YELLOW					6

CARNEGIE

YELLOW	2						
GREEN		4	2	12			
RED			2		4		2	4	2
BLACK					12		
BLUE						12	2	6

CHISHOLM

Sett (a) is an early tartan. Sett (b) originated in the *Vestiarium Scoticum*. Sett (c) is the hunting version of the *Vestiarium Scoticum* sett, with a brown ground replacing the red.

a)
RED	24			6	6	
BLUE		4	4			2
WHITE			2			
GREEN					16	

b)
RED	12	48					2
WHITE		4					
BLUE			12	2	2		
GREEN				4	4	24	

c)
BROWN	12	48					2
WHITE		4					
BLUE			12	2	2		
GREEN				4	4	24	

CLAN CHATTAN

RED	120				6	6		8	
BLACK		4				2		8	
WHITE			2	4			4		4
GREEN			32						
YELLOW					6		6		12
LT. BLUE								32	

CLARK (CLERGY)

BLUE	12			
BLACK		4	4	
GREEN			4	
RED				12

COCKBURN

GREEN	72	2	2						24	
BLACK		2	2	2	2	2	2	2		4
BLUE					24		24			
WHITE						2				
YELLOW								2		
RED										4

COLQUHOUN

Sett (a) is an early clan tartan dating from 18th century or earlier. Considered by some to be typical of those setts from the West coast and Islands. Sometimes the blue is replaced by purple

a)
BLUE	8	32				
BLACK		4		16		
WHITE			2			
GREEN					48	
RED						8

b)
BLUE	2	16				
BLACK		2	16			
WHITE			2			
GREEN				16		
RED					4	

COMYN, CUMMING

Sett (b) was recorded under this name in 1850, but had been in existence before then, and was recorded in 1831 as 'MacAulay'. Sett (c) was recorded in 1850, and approved then by the head of the family of Cumming. Sett (d), Cumming hunting, is unusual in that the black and blue stripes at the pivot point are always in the same order. It was used as the basis of the tartan of Gordonstoun School.

LT. BLUE	8		8					
BLACK		4		20				
ORANGE					2			
GREEN					20			
RED							8	8
a) WHITE						2		

BLACK	4							
RED		48		4		8		8
GREEN			8		8	16		16
b) WHITE							2	

BLACK	4				
RED		36	6		6
GREEN			12	18	18
c) WHITE					2

BLACK	2			12				16		2
RED		2	2		12	2		2		
GREEN			16			12				
d) BLUE					2				2	

N.B. Double band pivot

COOPER

This is a modern tartan.

RED	4										4
BLUE		4	64	2		4		8	8	4	
LAVENDER			8		8	8				8	
BLACK				4				26			
GREEN					20				4	68	

CRAIG

Designed in 1950 by John MacGregor Hastie, who attempted to represent the flecked grey of the granite crags typical in Scotland.

RED	2					6					2
BLACK		6	4	2	2		2	2		4	
GREEN			4				32		2		
GREY				4	6	4		36		4	
YELLOW									2		

CRANSTOUN, CRANSTON

A rare tartan, based on an illustration in *Vestiarium Scoticum*. It is described there as including two greens: 'that of a leaf of a tender ash tree, and the other the colour of grass'.

RED	4					
LT. GREEN		24				
BLUE			12	2	2	
GREEN				6	2	28

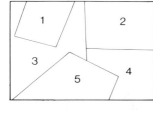

Photographs on pages 64 & 65
1. Cameron (clan)
2. Campbell of Argyll
3. Campbell of Breadalbane
4. Chisholm A.C.
5. Colquhoun

CRAWFORD
This sett first appeared in *Vestiarium Scoticum*.

DK. RED	12	60	6	6
WHITE		4		
GREEN			24	24

CRIEFF
See District Tartans page 172.

ROSE	4							4
RED	12	140	4	4	4		12	
GREEN		8	8		170	8		
PURPLE				42				

CUNNINGHAM
The tartan of a Lowland family, which first appeared in *Vestiarium Scoticum*. It is sometimes shown as a 'counterchange' pattern: one half of the mirror-repeat of the pattern being the opposite of the other.

WHITE	6			
RED		2	56	2
BLACK			2	60	6

DALZELL
This tartan was first illustrated in Logan's *Scottish Gael* 1831.

GREEN	12	4						64			
DK. RED		6									
RED			64		8		8		8	8	
BLUE				4		12		4		4	48
WHITE					2		2			2	

DAVIDSON
Sett (a) known as Davidson of Tulloch was certainly in use before 1822, when it was recorded in the collection of the Highland Society of London. Sett (b) is a more recent tartan.

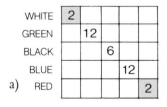

	WHITE	2				
	GREEN		12			
	BLACK			6		
	BLUE				12	
a)	RED					2

	RED	2							2
	BLUE		12	2					
	GREEN			2	16	16	2		
b)	BLACK					2	2	12	

DOUGLAS, green, DOUGLAS, grey
The Douglas family, originally from Lanarkshire, is classed as a Border clan and was one of the most powerful in Scotland. The grey Douglas (b) pattern is probably an old blanket pattern. The green (a) one was listed by Wilsons of Bannockburn in 1819 as 'No. 148'. The grey sett was first recorded in *Vestiarium Scoticum*.

	BLACK	8			
	LT. BLUE		4		
	GREEN			16	
	BLUE				16
a)	WHITE				2

	GREY	4	32	2	2	
b)	BLACK		2	16	2	32

67

DRUMMOND OF PERTH

Sett (a) was mentioned in a notebook of around 1800 as 'Perthshire Rock and Wheel'. It also appears in Wilsons Key Pattern Book in 1819. Traditionally, it was associated with the popular James Drummond, Duke of Perth, who fought in the '45, and died on board a French frigate while trying to escape, in the following year. Sett (b) was taken from the cloak worn by Prince Charles Edward, and which he left behind at Fingask Castle. See also Grant page 79.

a)
RED	72			16		
WHITE		2				2
BLUE			6		6	
YELLOW			2			
GREEN				32		
LT. BLUE					4	

b)
RED	96			16		
YELLOW		6			6	
BLUE			2			
GREEN				28		
LT. BLUE						8
WHITE						2

DUNBAR

The Dunbars were a very important Lowland family. This sett was first recorded in the *Vestiarium Scoticum*.

RED	8	56		12
BLACK		2	16	
GREEN				42

DUNBLANE

This tartan is first shown in a portrait of the 2nd Viscound Dunblane, who died in 1729. This does not necessarily mean it is a Dunblane district tartan, but it is certainly associated with this name.

WHITE	2		2	2	2	2	
BLUE		4					
RED			30				
GREEN				4	10	4	12
YELLOW						10	

DUNCAN

First illustrated in Johnson, 1906.

BLACK	8			
GREEN		42	42	
WHITE			6	
BLUE				42
RED				8

Photographs on pages 68 & 69
1. Comyn
2. Cranston
3. Cunningham
4. Davidson A.C.
5. Douglas (green)

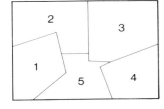

DUNDAS

This sett first appeared in the *Vestiarium Scoticum*.

BLACK	4			24	8
GREEN		4	48		
RED			2		
BLUE					32

DYCE

BLUE	18	2	2						16
BLACK		2	2	16		2		16	
GREEN					16		16		
YELLOW					2	2			
WHITE									2

ELLIOT

The tartan of a Border family. This appeared in the *Vestiarium Scoticum*. (See poem on spelling page 52.)

RED	2		
BLUE		6	32
BROWN		8	

ERSKINE

The tartan of a Lowland family, first recorded in *Vestiarium Scoticum*. This is one of the simple old blanket patterns and found throughout the Highlands. There is also a black and white colouring of the same sett, and the sett of Erskine hunting is in two shades of green.

RED	8	56	2	
GREEN		2	48	12

FARQUHARSON

The Farquharson tartan was recorded before 1820, and sett (a) is thought to be older. Both setts are based on that of the Black Watch.

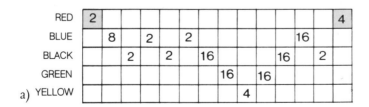

a)

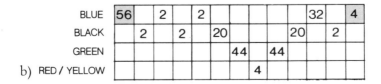

b)

FERGUSON OF ATHOL

Sett (a) is identical to that of the Maclaren, who were followers of the Murrays of Atholl, along with the Athol Fergusons. Sett (b) is an earlier, more primitive, tartan, which is asymmetric. It is referred to as 'Ferguson' in the Cockburn Collection, made before 1820.

BLUE	48					
BLACK		16		2		
GREEN			16	16		
RED				4		
a) WHITE						4

LT. GREEN	10		
BLUE		12	
b) RED			2

N.B. *This sett is asymmetric.*

FERGUSON OF BALQUIHIDDER

An original pattern from Wilsons of Bannockburn.

GREEN	4		24	
BLUE		24		
RED		2		
BLACK			24	4

FLETCHER, FLETCHER OF DUNANS, FLESHER

This sett (Fletcher) is of comparatively recent origin. An earlier version known as Fletcher of Dunans, with a red pivot line instead of black, was illustrated in 1906.

BLUE	12		12		
BLACK		2		16	4
RED				2	
GREEN					16

FORBES

This tartan is said to have been designed in 1822, for the family of Forbes of Pitsligo, by a Miss Forbes. The design resembles the regimental Gordon, but with the yellow line changed to white. It is very similar to the Lamont (page 87) which was once in commercial production under the name of Forbes, and shown in a manufacturer's catalogue of 1819.

BLUE	16		4		4					16	4
BLACK		2		2		12	2	2	12		2
GREEN							16		16		
WHITE								4			

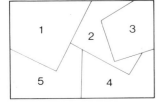

Photographs on pages 72 & 73
1. Drummond of Perth
2. Duncan
3. Elliot
4. Erskine
5. Farquharson

FORBES, dress

BLUE	4	16						6	4
BLACK		4	16	2		2	16		
GREEN				24		24			
WHITE					4			6	28	4

FORSYTH

BLACK	8		32	
GREEN		44		
YELLOW			4	
BLUE				36
RED				8

FRASER

Sett (a), one of the Red Frasers, is the most popular of the Fraser tartans, but there is some doubt as to its attribution as a Fraser sett. Sett (b) is an older tartan of the Clan Fraser. The hunting version (c) is comparatively modern, and created by substituting brown for the conspicuous red of the Red Fraser sett.

a)

WHITE	2			
RED		24	2	2
GREEN			12	
BLUE				12

b)

BLUE	32	2					24	2
RED		2	2	32	32		2	
GREEN				24	4	24		

c)

WHITE / RED	2			
BROWN	24			
GREEN		12		
RED			2	2
BLUE			12	

FRASER OF LOVAT

This sett is similar to that of Clan Fraser, with the substitution of a white line for the green one on the red ground.

BLUE	32	2					24	2
RED		2	2	32	32		2	
GREEN				24		24		
WHITE					4			

HAMILTON

	WHITE	RED		BLUE	
	2				
		18	2		
				12	12

Rows: WHITE, RED, BLUE

HAMILTON, hunting

	WHITE	GREEN		BLUE	
	2				
		18	2		
				12	12

Rows: WHITE, GREEN, BLUE

HAY and LEITH

Hay is the family name of the Earls of Errol, and the tartan (b) is used also by the family of Leith. It was recorded in the Wilson Key Pattern book of 1819 as 'Leith Tartan'. Sett (a) was first shown in the *Vestiarium Scoticum* and is one of the most elaborate there – possibly because the Sobieski brothers (see page 24) had at one time used the name of Hay. (See also Leith pages, 88 & 89.)

a)

WHITE	12									
RED		4	4	96	4	4			12	
BLACK			2							
GREEN				8	24	4	72	8		
YELLOW								4		

b)

BLACK	6		4					30				4		6
RED		2		32	2	4			2	4	2	32		2
YELLOW			2			2				2			2	
GREEN				4				30						
WHITE									2					
PURPLE											30		4	

HENDERSON or MACKENDRICK

YELLOW	2					
BLACK		12	2			
GREEN			8	32	8	
BLUE					2	12
WHITE						2

HOME

BLUE	6	48				
GREEN			4			
BLACK				16	4	56
RED					2	2

HUNTER

GREEN	16	16					
BLACK			2	16			16
RED					2		2
BLUE					16	16	
WHITE						2	

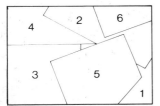

Photographs on pages 80 & 81
1. Gordon
2. Gow A.C.
3. Graham of Menteith
4. Graham of Montrose
5. Grant
6. Gunn

HUNTLY

GREEN	16	16	4	4															16	16
RED		4	24	6	24	6		6		6	24	2		2	24	2		2	24	4
WHITE					2					2										
YELLOW						2		2												
BLUE							24		24				2	4	2		2	4	2		

INGLES, INGLIS

WHITE	8				
GREEN		56			
BLUE			36		36
RED				8	
YELLOW					6

INNES, MACINNES

Sett (a) is that of the Innes of the Moray district, and (b) is the sett for the MacInnes, of the West. The two clans are not connected, but the tartans are similar. Tartan (b) was known, and recorded, in 1843.

a)

LT. BLUE	6								
BLACK		24	4		4			4	4
RED			4	4	24	6	6		6
YELLOW						4			
BLUE							12		
GREEN								20	
WHITE									4

b)

YELLOW	4							
BLACK		24	4	4	6	6		
GREEN			4	4	32			12
LT. BLUE						6		
BLUE							24	
RED								4

INVERNESS

RED	144				36
BLUE		12	22		
WHITE			4		
GREEN				4	4
BLACK				4	

IRVINE

GREEN	72			
BLUE		36	4	
BLACK			4	
WHITE				4

JOHNSTONE, JOHNSTON

YELLOW	6					
GREEN		4	60			
BLACK			2		4	4
BLUE				48	4	

KEITH and AUSTIN

BLACK	4		8	
GREEN		18		
BLUE			8	8

KENNEDY

This tartan, said by some to have been worn by the Northern branch of the Kennedy family in Lochaber, was later adopted by the Kennedys of Carrick in the 18th century, as a sign of their Jacobite sympathies.

RED	4											
GREEN		48					24	4		6		4
BLUE			8	6		6	8					
BLACK			6		6		6					4
PURPLE								2	2			
YELLOW											2	

KERR, CARR

The Border Kerrs were the best-known family of this name, so were unlikely to have had a tartan until this one appeared in the *Vestiarium Scoticum*. There is a more recent hunting sett in which the red is changed to a dark blue.

BLACK	8		2		28		2		2	
RED		4		56						
GREEN						6		4		40

KIDD, KID, KYDD

RED	36	36						36		10
LT. BLUE		10			20	6	20			
GREEN			48							
YELLOW				6						
BLACK				38	6	6			10	
WHITE								8		

KILGOUR

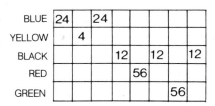

BLUE	24		24				
YELLOW		4					
BLACK			12		12		12
RED				56			
GREEN						56	

N.B. This sett is asymmetric.

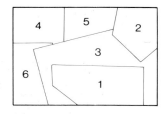

Photographs on pages 84 & 85
1. Hamilton
2. Hay
3. Home
4. Hunter A.C.
5. Johnstone
6. Keith & Austin

KINCAID
A simple modern tartan designed for the Chief and recorded with the Lord Lyon in 1960.

BLACK	22		
GREEN		34	
RED			6

LAMOND, LAMONT
This tartan is identical to the Forbes tartan allowing the difference of the black guards to the white line.

BLUE	6		2		2				8		2
BLACK		2		2		8			8		2	
GREEN							8		8			
WHITE								2				

LAUDER
When the Sobieski brothers 'prepared' the *Vestiarium Scoticum*, one of their great friends was Sir Thomas Dick Lauder, and this Lauder tartan made its first appearance in that book.

RED	4				
GREEN		30		6		6
BLACK			8			
BLUE					16	

LEITH
See Hay and Leith.

LENNOX
See District Tartans page 173.

RED	4	20			
DK. RED		2	4		
GREY GREEN				20	4
WHITE					2	

MACALPINE

Macalpine is not the name of a single clan, but of a group of clans, (MacGregor, Grant, Mackinnon, MacQuarrie, MacNab, MacFie and MacAulay). The tartan is basically green, whereas the tartans of the component clans are red-based. It is of comparatively recent origin.

GREEN	2			2	12		12		2		
BLACK		8				2		2		8	8
YELLOW			2								
BLUE				8	2						
WHITE										2	

N.B. This sett is asymmetric.

MACARTHUR

Some families of the MacArthurs were linked, at various times, with the MacDonalds. This could explain the similarity of this sett to that of MacDonald, Lord of the Isles. This tartan was recorded in the *Vestiarium Scoticum,* but there is possibly an older sett in the Highland Society of London collection.

YELLOW	6			
GREEN		60	12	
BLACK			24	64

MACAULY

This tartan was well established in 1881, when it was recorded. An extended version had appeared before that date, in 1831, but this is now known as Comyn.

BLACK	4			
RED		32	6	
GREEN			12	16
WHITE				2

MACAULAY, hunting

This is a modern sett, based on the earlier MacAulay (now known as Comyn).

RED	4					
GREEN		24	16			12
BLACK			8	32	32	
WHITE					2	

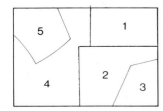

Photographs on pages 92 & 93
1. Leslie
2. Red Leslie
3. Lindsay
4. Logan & MacLennan
5. MacAlister

MACBEAN, MACBAIN

The MacBeans are often shown in portraits as wearing the Clan Mackintosh tartan (although they are a minor sept of Clan Chattan). This sett was registered comparatively recently, under the name of MacBain. A piece of the MacBean/MacBain tartan went to the moon and back in Apollo XII in November 1969 with Commander Alan L. Bean, the US astronaut (see page 182) and it is now in the Tartan Museum at Comrie.

RED	120							10		10		
WHITE		4		4		4		4			4	
LT. BLUE			10		10							
BLACK			4	4		4	4					
GREEN							24			4		20
DK. RED									10	10		

MACBETH

This is a version of the Royal Stuart, with a blue ground instead of the red. It is thought that the name was attached after the name 'Macbeth' was seen to have royal connections.

BLUE	72						
YELLOW		8					
BLACK			12	2	2		2
WHITE				2	2			2
GREEN						16	
RED						12	6

MACCALLUM, MACCULLUM (see also MALCOLM)

Sett (a) is an early tartan, but, as with most setts, difficult to date precisely. It was certainly recorded in the Collection of the Highland Society of London in 1822. Set (b) is more recent, dating from the middle of the 19th century.

a)

BLACK	2		12		4	
BLUE		12				
GREEN				8		16
LT. BLUE					2	

b)

BLACK	2		12			12
BLUE		12				
GREEN				12	12	
RED					2	

MACCOLL

The MacColls descended from the MacDonalds, and this sett bears a distinct resemblance to their tartans. It is thought to have been in commercial production during the 18th century, but may not have called MacColl until 1830.

GREEN	8		2					16			
RED		2		24	2		2		4	2	24
BLUE					2	6	2			2	

MACDERMOT, MACDIARMID

BLACK	24		56		2		2	
RED		4						8
GREEN				24		24		
WHITE						6		

MACDONALD, clan

Possibly derived from an early Lochaber district tartan, which area has been dominated by the MacDonald's, their adherents and successors after the break-up of the MacDonald Lordship of the Isles in 1493.

GREEN	16	4	24					
RED		2	6		2	6	2	
BLACK				24	24			
BLUE							4	16

MACDONALD OF ARDNAMURCHAN

Also known as MacDonald of Glencoe.

RED	8	8	24	
BLACK		16	16	2
YELLOW				4

MACDONALD OF BOISDALE

First appeared in the Cockburn Collection of 1815.

RED	32			8		8		48		12		32
WHITE		2	2						2		2	2	2
BLUE			12						64		12		
LT. GREEN				2	2	2	2						
GREEN					12		32						

MACDONALD OF CLANRANALD

First recorded in the Cockburn Collection of 1815.

GREEN	12	4	22					
RED		4	6		4	6	4	
WHITE				4				
BLACK				22				
BLUE						24	4	12

MACDONALD OF GLENALADALE

One of the few asymmetric tartans. It was found in Prince Edward Island, Canada, and said to have been taken there by the migrating MacDonalds in 1772.

BLUE	56		10				
RED		52		52	10		10
WHITE			4	4		4	
GREEN					56		

N.B. This sett is asymmetric.

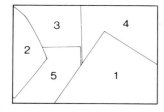

Photographs on pages 96 & 97
1. Macalpine
2. Macarthur
3. Macaulay
4. Macbeth
5. Maccallum

MACDONALD OF GLENGARRY
Was also recorded in the Cockburn Collection of 1815.

BLUE	16	4	24					
RED		2	6	2		6	2	
BLACK				24				
GREEN					24	4	8	
WHITE								2

MACDONALD OF KEPPOCH
This sett was taken from a plaid given to Prince Charles Edward by The Keppoch who led his clan in the '45 rising. (This chief was ashamed of the MacDonalds when they were reluctant to charge the Hanoverian army at Culloden, and crying 'My God! Have the children of my tribe deserted me?' dashed forward on the enemy to be immediately shot down by them.)

GREEN	4				24	
RED		4	48		6	8
BLUE			2	12		2
LT. GREEN				2		

MACDONALD OF KINGSBURGH
This tartan sett was taken from the fragment which was the only remains of a waistcoat given to Prince Charles Edward by Alexander MacDonald of Kingsburgh after Culloden. The colours were too bright for a fugitive, and the Prince exchanged it with one worn by Malcolm MacLeod. MacLeod, in danger of capture, hid the waistcoat in the cleft of a rock. Returning a year later, after his release, he found that only a fragment had survived the exposure (see page 20).

RED	6		36			
GREEN		6		42	2	
YELLOW			2		2	6
WHITE				2		

MACDONALD, LORD OF THE ISLES
The red sett was first illustrated circa 1750 in the portrait of the MacDonald boys by Jeremiah Davidson.

BLACK	4		
RED		36	10
GREEN			4	32

MACDONALD, LORD OF THE ISLES, hunting

GREEN	48	4						
WHITE		2	4	2	2	4	2	
BLUE				4	24	4	4	24

MACDONALD OF SLEAT

GREEN	32	4	
RED		10	72

MACDOUGAL

Sett (a) there is some controversy about the colour of the fine lines in this sett. It dates from the early 19th century. Sett (d) was first recorded in *Vestiarium Scoticum*.

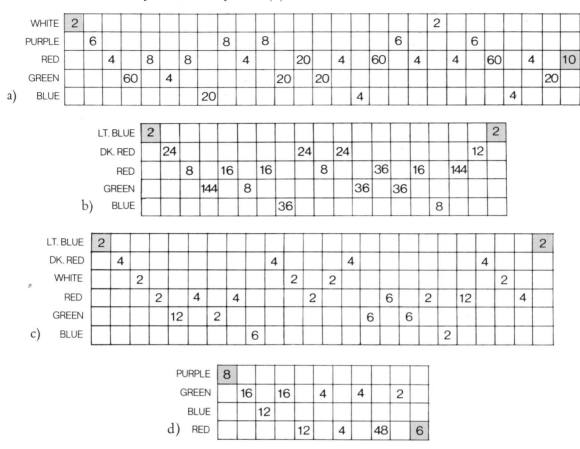

MACDUFF

Sett (a), this tartan, recorded in the late 19th century, is similar to the Royal Stuart (minus the white and yellow) and may have been designed as an indication of the links between the MacDuffs (Earls of Fife) and the Crown. Sett (b) was first recorded in the *Vestiarium Scoticum*. Sett (c) the hunting sett, is of comparatively recent origin.

MACDUFF, dress

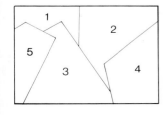

Photographs on pages 100 & 101
1. MacDonald (clan)
2. MacDonald of Clanranald
3. MacDonald of Glengarry
4. MacDonald, Lord of the Isles (hunting)
5. MacDonald of Keppoch

MACEWEN, MACEWAN

This clan was broken up before the 16th century by the Campbells, and the tartan is similar to the Campbell of Loudon sett. It was first recorded in 1906.

YELLOW/RED	4				
BLACK		2	24	2	
GREEN			24		
BLUE				24	4

MACFARLANE

'Wild MacFarlan's plaided clan' is a branch of the ancient Celtic Earls of Lennox, with lands around Arrochar, Loch Lomond. The sett (a) was first recorded in the Wilson List in 1819 and is a direct colour change on another in the list, called Mackintosh (now called Clan Chattan). Sett (b) was first recorded in *Vestiarium Scoticum*. Sett (c) is the hunting sett.

a)

RED	84			6		6		6	
BLACK		2		2			8		
GREEN			24			4			6
WHITE				4		4		8	
PURPLE						24			

b)

BLACK	14		2	
WHITE			12	12

c)

GREEN	84	24				4			6
BLACK		2		2			8		
WHITE			4		4			8	
RED			6	6			6		
BLUE						24			

MACFIE, MACPHEE

Ths design is of comparatively recent origin.

a)

WHITE/YELLOW	2			
RED		24	2	
GREEN			4	32

b)

WHITE	2					
RED		24	2		2	24
GREEN			4	32	4	
YELLOW						2

MACGILLIVRAY

The MacGillivrays came from Morven and Strathnairn, and the light blue lines are found in many tartans of these areas, strengthening the theory that it was weavers who were the original creators of tartans, making alterations to suit different clans and families.

RED	8		64	4	4		8	8
LT. BLUE		2		4				2
BLUE			2		24				4
GREEN						32		

MACGREGOR

Sett (a) was once called MacGregor Murray, and it has been consistently recorded since the early 19th century. Sett (b) seems to have acquired the name Rob Roy at the beginning of the 19th century when Wilsons were turning out patterns with heroic names e.g. Wellington, Robin Hood etc. The MacGregors seem to have accepted the Rob Roy sett as being long-founded, and it has been a popular cloth for trews.

a)

RED	72		8		
GREEN		36		12	
BLACK					2
WHITE					4

b)

RED	2	
BLACK		2

MACGREGOR, hunting

GREY	10				
BLACK		4			
GREEN			28	68	
DK. RED				24	160

MACHARDY

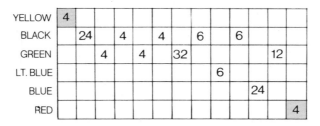

BLUE	2		12		12	
RED		2				2
GREEN			12			2
WHITE				2		

MACINNES

See Innes' page 83.

YELLOW	4								
BLACK		24	4	4		6	6		
GREEN			4	4	32			12	
LT. BLUE						6			
BLUE								24	
RED									4

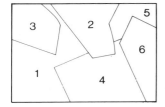

Photographs on pages 104 & 105
1. Macdougal
2. Macduff
3. MacEwen
4. MacFarlane
5. MacFie
6. MacGillivray

MACIVER

The similarity of this sett to that of the MacArthurs in interesting, because their lands were on opposite sides of Loch Fyne. The change of colour of the grounds only is another indication of the original sett being planned by a weaver in the area. It is recorded that, at the Battle of Culloden, the MacIvers were placed so that they would not face the Argyl men, who wore the same tartan. If so, the MacIvers were, at that time, wearing either Black Watch (Campbell) or the simpler Campbell of Cawdor Pattern.

WHITE / YELLOW	2			
RED		24		4
BLACK			4	32

MACKAY

The lands of the MacKays and the Gunns were adjacent, and their tartans were very alike. This sett was first recorded in the Wilson List of 1819. The blue in this sett was sometimes described as 'corbeau' (French: crow), a very dark green, nearly black.

BLACK	6		28		
GREEN		28		4	6
BLUE					28

MACKEANE, MACIAIN

The MacKeane sett is the 'opposite' of the MacQueen, and both originatd in the *Vestiarium Scoticum*. It is thought that this was a 'pun' conceived by the Sobieski brothers on the similarity of the two names. Both MacKeanes and MacQueens derived from the MacDonalds.

YELLOW	4				
BLACK		2	16	16	
RED			24	8	8

MACKELLAR

GREEN	60	8		8	12				
WHITE		6			6				8
YELLOW			10						
BLACK						28	28		
LT. BLUE						6			
BLUE								36	

MACKENZIE

BLUE	24		4		4				24	
BLACK		4		4		24	2	2	24	2
GREEN						24		24		
WHITE							4			
RED										4

MACKINLAY

This sett was recorded in Johnson's (1906), and is similar to Murray or Urquhart.

BLUE	4	16						4	4	12
BLACK		4		12	2	2	12	4	4	
GREEN			16				16			
RED					4					

MACKINNON

This is the clan tartan authorized by the Chief, but several variations existed before this ruling.

WHITE	4								
RED		8		32		4	12	6	
PURPLE			4						4
GREEN				16	4		32	4	
BLUE					8			4	

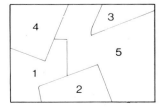

Photographs on pages 108 & 109
1. MacGregor
2. MacGregor, Rob Roy
3. MacInnes
4. Mackay
5. Mackay Strathnaver

MACKINTOSH, clan

This is one of the few tartans that can be associated with the name of its clan from before the '45 rising.

RED	44	4	6	
BLUE		10		2
GREEN			22	

THE MACKINTOSH (Chief)

This tartan is very similar to Clan Chattan.

RED	48				4	4			6	
BLACK		2				2		4		
WHITE			2	2				2		2
GREEN			12							
YELLOW					4		4		6	
LT. BLUE							12			

MACKINTOSH, hunting

This is recorded at the Lyon Court.

YELLOW	4				
GREEN		24		24	
BLUE			12		2
RED				6	8

MACINTYRE and GLENORCHY

The MacIntyres never became a clan. Sett (a) is sometimes regarded as a district tartan, and occasionally referred to as just 'Glenorchy'. Sett (b) was first known in the *Vestiarium Scoticum,* and is now known as the hunting MacIntyre. Sett (c) is the same as sett (a) with a very large repeat. It is described as 'Cumming, Glenorchy' and was recorded in the early 19th century.

a)

BLACK	4									
GREEN		4		12				36		4
RED			6	4	8		6		6	
BLUE			36				12			
LT. BLUE						2				
BLACK									4	

b)

WHITE	8				
GREEN		64			8
BLUE			24	24	
RED				6	

c)

GREEN	66			24					24			44	
RED		6		16	6	6		6	6	16		6	6	
BLUE			24			40	6		40			24		6
LT. BLUE				2				2			2			

MACLACHLAN

Sett (a) dates from at least 1830, but it is thought to have been a neglected design dating from much earlier, and is considered to be one of the finest of the old clan setts. Sett (b) is an old tartan, recorded in the early 19th century, alongside a simple check of red and green, (originally called MacLachlan, but now adopted by the Moncreiffs, and formally abandoned by the MacLachlans.) Sett (c) is the *Vestiarium Scoticum* sett, said then to be that worn by the MacLachlan of MacLachlan.

a)
RED	32		4		4				32	4
BLACK		4		4		32		32		4
BLUE						32	32			
GREEN							6			

b)
YELLOW	6			6	
WHITE		4			4
BLACK			32		
GREEN				32	
RED					48

c)
YELLOW	12	48	4		4	
BLACK		4	12	42	12

MACLAINE OF LOCHBUIE

Sett (a) is an old one, dating from at least the 18th century, and is recorded in many collections. Sett (b) is the hunting tartan, and was called 'modern' in records of 1893, therefore probably dates from the mid-19th century.

a)
RED	64		
GREEN		16	
LT. BLUE			8
YELLOW				2

b)
BLUE	64	8	
RED		6	
BLACK			2
YELLOW				6

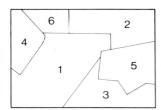

Photographs on pages 112 & 113
1. Mackenzie
2. Mackinlay
3. Mackinnon
4. Mackintosh (clan)
5. MacIntyre

MACLAREN

This sett, now known as MacLaren, had been produced commercially for many years at the beginning of the 19th century by Wilsons of Bannockburn as pattern No. 232, later called 'Regent'. When George IV succeeded to the throne in 1820, the name became out-of-date, and the sett was then called MacLaren, and continued in production.

BLUE	48				
BLACK		16		2	
GREEN			16	16	
RED				4	
YELLOW					4

MACLEAN OF DUART

Sett (a) was recorded in a collection in the early 19th century. It is a variation on the Royal Stuart pattern. Sett (b) – the hunting MacLean – is thought to be one of the oldest setts, said to date back to the 16th century. It is first illustrated as 'MacLean' in the *Vestiarium Scoticum,* but there are records of a rent payable by MacLeans in 1587 of 'sexty ells of cloth of white, black and green colours', which would indicate an earlier date.

BLACK	2			2		2	6	
RED		4	24					
LT. BLUE			2				2	
GREEN				16				
WHITE								
BLUE						2		8
a) YELLOW						2		

BLACK	2		4	12		12	
GREEN		32	4				6
b) WHITE					2		

MACLENNON
See Logan.

MACLEOD
Sett (a) was recorded in the early 19th century. It is sometimes called hunting MacLeod and is of the basic design common to the early tartans originating in the Islands and the West. (MacLeod of Assynt is similar, but without the black edges to the yellow overcheck.) Sett (b) first appeared in the *Vestiarium Scoticum:* 'MacLeod' was one of the 'particular friends' of the Sobieski brothers.

a)
RED	6				
BLACK		4	20	4	
GREEN			30		
BLUE				40	
YELLOW					4

b)
RED	2			
YELLOW		24	2	
BLACK			16	16

MACLINTOCK

GREEN	72	6						
RED			6	6	6	80	6	12
BLUE					18		6	4
LT. BLUE						4		

MACMILLAN
Sett (b), the modern hunting MacMillan, was designed by taking the red and yellow from sett (a) and using them as an overcheck on the blue/black/green of conventional dark tartan.

a)
RED	2		4		6	24	6
YELLOW		16		16		4		2	

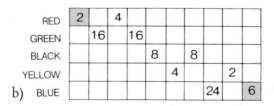

b)
RED	2	4					
GREEN		16	16				
BLACK				8	8		
YELLOW					4		2	
BLUE							24	6

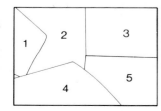

Photographs on pages 116 & 117
1. MacLachlan A.C.
2. MacLaine of Lochbuie
3. MacLaren A.C.
4. MacLean of Duart
5. Hunting MacLean

MACNAB

Sett (a), the usual Macnab tartan, was recorded in the early 19th century. It is identical in proportions to the Black Watch, but with very different colours. Sett (b) was said to have been designed for the Chief, and to be 'an old pattern, reckoned appropriate to this clan'. It was recorded in the Wilson List in 1819. Sett (c) was first recorded in the *Vestiarium Scoticum*.

a)
	GREEN	DK. RED	RED
	16		
		2	
	2	2	
		12	
			16
		12	16
		2	
	14		
	2		

b)
	DK. RED	GREEN	LT. BLUE	RED
	48			
		2		
		4	2	
				48

c)
	BLACK	RED	DK. RED	GREEN
	2			
		24		
			4	
			4	8
		4		
				12

MACNAUGHTON

The fine lines in this design are thought by some authorities to have been a mistake, perpetuated in many subsequent records. First recorded by Logan in *The Scottish Gael* in 1831.

	BLACK	LT. BLUE	RED	GREEN
	2			
		2		
		16	32	
	24			
				32
		2	32	
	2			

MACNEIL

Although sett (a) is the most popular MacNeil tartan, sett (b) has been described as the oldest of several known Clan MacNeil tartans.

a)

	1	2	3	4	5
YELLOW	6				
BLACK		4	24		
GREEN			24		
BLUE				28	
WHITE					6

b)

	1	2	3	4	5	6
YELLOW	2					
BLACK		6	28			
GREEN			30			
BLUE				32		
RED					4	
WHITE						2

MACNEIL OF BARRA

	1	2	3	4	5
WHITE	2				
BLUE		10			
BLACK			24	24	
GREEN				24	
YELLOW					2

MACNEIL OF COLONSAY

This is probably of a later date than other MacNeil setts.

	1	2	3	4	5
BLACK	4	12			
BLUE		12			8
GREEN			12	12	
WHITE			2		

MACNICOL, NICHOLSON

There would appear to be no definite early tartan for the MacNicols. (They would probably have used that of the MacLeods.) This sett derived from a mid-19th century drawing of a 'MacNicol woman wearing a shawl'.

	1	2	3	4	5	6	7	8
BLACK	4			16	12			4
RED		20	20			4	20	20
GREEN			4			26	4	
LT. BLUE					4			

MACORQUDALE

The same sett as the Campbell of Cawdor tartan but with different shades of blue and green, deliberately differencing the pattern.

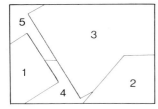

Photographs on pages 120 & 121
1. Macleod of Harris (hunting)
2. Macmillan (dress)
3. Old Macmillan
4. Macnab
5. Macnaughton A.C.

MACPHAIL

a)
BLACK	8		28	
LT. BLUE		4		
GREEN		52		
RED			12	100

b)
RED	4				
BLUE		46			
BLACK		28	4		
GREEN				32	
WHITE					4

MACPHEE
See Macfie.

MACPHERSON
Sett (a), the Clan Macpherson, was being woven commercially by Wilsons of Bannockburn at the beginning of the 19th century and was sometimes called 'Kidd', 'Caledonian', or 'No. 43'. Sett (b) is a more modern version (also Clan MacPherson) with less red and a smaller repeat. Sett (c), the hunting tartan, is thought to have been the earliest to have been worn by the Clan. It has also been recorded with a white ground.

a)
RED	2		24						24	24
BLACK		2			2		2	12		
WHITE				2						
LT. BLUE					8	2	8		4	
YELLOW								2		
GREEN									16	

b)
RED	2		8						12	12
BLACK		2			2		2	12		
WHITE				2						
BLUE					8	4	8		2	
YELLOW								2		
GREEN									16	

c)
BLUE	2			2		2
RED		2	2		2	2
GREY			16			
BLACK					16	

MACQUARRIE
Sett (a) is the most popular MacQuarrie tartan today; it has been recorded since the late 19th century. Sett (b) is said to be authentic.

a)
RED	32		2		8	
GREEN		2		2		24

b)
RED	2	12		2		2	12	2
LT. BLUE			2					2
BLUE					6			2
GREEN						12	12	

MACQUEEN
The MacQueens are dependants of the MacDonalds and this sett was first shown in the *Vestiarium Scoticum*.

YELLOW	2			
BLACK		24	4		4
RED			12	12	

MACRAE

Sett (a) is the most popular MacRae tartan. Sett (b), the hunting MacRae, is based on a piece of kilt believed to have been worn at Sheriffmuir. Sett (c), MacRae of Conchra, was based on the design of a piece of early 18th-century knitted hose, said to have been worn in battle. This sett is sometimes known as dress MacRae.

a)

GREEN	8	8													2	2	8	8
RED		2	8	2	2	8	2	2	8	2	2	2	8	2	8	2		
BLUE			2	2	2	2	2	2		8	8							
WHITE							2					2						

b)

WHITE	6					
BLACK		2	28		4	
PURPLE			30			
GREY/GREEN				8	8	28
DK. RED				4		

c)

YELLOW	2		
LT. BLUE		10	
WHITE		10	
RED			2

MACTAGGART

BLUE	2	12			
RED		2			
BLACK			12		
GREEN				2	18
LT. BLUE				4	

MACTAVISH

Some MacTavishes wear the tartan of Campbell of Argyll (page 62). This sett is also used by the Thomsons (Thomson is the anglicized form of Mactavish.)

LT. BLUE	4		12	2
RED		24		
BLUE			4	
BLACK				12

MACTHOMAS

This is thought to be a modern family tartan, recorded with the Tartan Society in 1963 by Captain MacThomas. There are, however, opinions that it might date from as early as 1795.

BLUE	6	42			
DK. RED		4		4	
BLACK			22		
GREEN				42	6

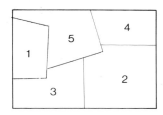

Photographs on pages 124 & 125
1. MacNeil of Barra A.C.
2. Hunting MacNicol
3. MacPherson
4. MacQuarrie
5. MacQueen

MAITLAND

This tartan was designed in 1953, and was worn in that year by standard bearers in Queen Elizabeth II's Coronation procession. It was registered at Lyon Court in 1960. It should be noted that this is a restricted tartan, and should not be worn or woven by anyone without the permission of the Chief.

RED	4						
YELLOW		4	4				
BLUE			4			16	
GREEN					18	6	6
BLACK					8		

MALCOLM (see MACCULLUM)

Although 'Malcolm' is a variation of MacCullum, this sett is always known as Malcolm. It is one of the few asymmetric tartans. First illustrated in Smith's book of 1850. As with other asymmetric setts, it is thought to have originated from an attempt to produce an earlier sett from memory.

BLUE	2	12							12	
RED		2								2
BLACK			12	2		2		2	12	
GREEN				12				12		
YELLOW						2				
LT. BLUE							2			

N.B. This sett is asymmetric.

MAR TRIBE

The Mars are not a clan, but a Pictish tribe. This tartan is also known as Skene (See also District Tartans page 172) and is registered at Lyon Court.

RED	2			
BLACK		4	4	
GREEN		32		
YELLOW				2

MARSHALL

Wears 'Keith & Austin' tartan.

MATHESON

Sett (a) is the most popular Matheson tartan recorded. First illustrated in Smith's book of 1850. Sett (b) is the more recent hunting version, in which the conspicous red is directly replaced by blue.

a)
GREEN	16		2		2			8		2		8		2		2		16		8
RED		8		2		48			2		2		16		2		2		4	
BLUE							16											16		

b)
GREEN	16		2		2			8		2		8		2		2		16		8
BLUE		8		2		48			2		2		16		2		2		4	
BLACK							16											16		

MAXWELL

A Lowland tartan, first recorded in the *Vestiarium Scoticum*.

RED	6		56		8		6
GREEN		2				32	
BLACK				12			

MELVILLE

BLACK	4		26		8
BLUE		24			
GREEN				36	
WHITE			4		

MENZIES

Sett (a) is reputedly based on a knitted hose pattern. It was said to have attracted attention in 1842 'on the occasion of Her Majesty's visit'. It is now more popular in the hunting version, sett (b) colours. It is also made in black and white, sett (c). The oldest of the Menzies tartans is shown in sett (d), but this is rarely used.

a)
RED	72		6		12		2	
WHITE		8		8		4		24

b)
GREEN	96		4		12		6	
RED		8		8		4		18

c)
BLACK	64		4		8		2	
WHITE		8		8		4		12

d)
RED	10			10
LT. BLUE		4		
WHITE			2	
GREEN			10	

MIDDLETON

A tartan similar to that of MacDonald Lord of the Isles, but with different proportions.

GREEN	128		16	
RED		8		88

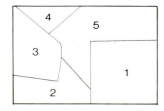

Photographs on pages 128 & 129
1. Macrae A.C.
2. MacTaggart A.C.
3. MacTavish
4. Malcolm
5. Marr

MITCHELL
See Galbraith, Hunter, Russell.

MOFFAT

BLACK	2					
RED		4	16	24	2	128
BLUE		4			2	32
GREEN				32		

MONCREIFFE (see MACLACHLAN)
A very old pattern of simple design. All rights in this tartan were vested in the Chief of the Moncreiffes, Sir Iain Moncreiffe of that Ilk, by Madam MacLachlan of MacLachlan, the Chief of the MacLachlans. It was suitable for the Moncreiffes because it did incorporate the colours of the Moncreiffe 'red lion rampant', and their badge of oak leaves and acorns.

RED	2		2
GREEN		2	

MONTGOMERY, MONTGOMERIE
This early tartan is said to have been adopted by the Montgomeries of Ayrshire around 1707 and, as such, would be one of the earliest authentic Lowland patterns. At the end of the 16th century, Lady Montgomery of Eglinton was encouraging the weaving of tartan in Ireland, and setting up woollen and linen mills there.

BLACK	8		8		8
GREEN		10			
PURPLE			56		
RED				10	

MORGAN
This sett was illustrated in the *Vestiarium Scoticum*. It is also known as 'Blue Mackay'.

BLUE	4		4	32
BLACK		12	12	
RED				2

MORRISON

Sett (a) was taken from the cover of an old family bible, and registered at Lyon Court in 1967. Sett (b) was illustrated in Johnson (1906) and is adding a red line to that of Mackay (a neighbouring clan). This is the tartan of the Clan Morrison Society.

a)

GREEN	10				30	18
RED		64	14	34		
BLACK			10	10		
WHITE					8	

b)

BLACK	6		28		
GREEN		28		4	
BLUE					28
RED					6

MOWAT, MOWATT

First recorded in Johnson's book of 1906, this tartan is similar to that of Campbell of Breadalbane.

BLUE	36	4			
BLACK		2	36		32
YELLOW				4	
GREEN					32

MUIR

BLUE	120						
BLACK		30					2
GREEN			20	20	20	20	
RED				4	4	4	
YELLOW							8

MUNRO

Sett (a) was woven by Wilsons as 'Lochiel', and is in an early 19th-century collection as 'Cameron of Lochiel', later becoming 'Munro'. Some early samples show the dark red stripes as bright pink. Sett (b) was first shown in the *Vestiarium Scoticum*. For everyday use, the clan wears the Black Watch, and it has been claimed that this was an early Munro tartan (see Campbell, page 62).

a)

GREEN	4	4						32		
DK. RED		4								
RED			32		6		6		6	6	48
BLUE				2		12		2		2	
YELLOW					2		2			2	

b)

WHITE	6		
RED		64	8
BLACK			36	36

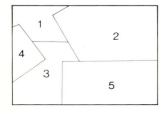

Photographs on pages 132 & 133
1. Matheson
2. Maxwell
3. Menzies (hunting)
4. Montgomery A.C.
5. Ancient Montgomery

MURRAY OF ATHOL

This sett may have been a district tartan, possibly named Athol before it was called Murray. It has also been referred to as 'Murray of Mansfield'. It was first recorded in the early 19th century, and is based on the Black Watch, with one red line replacing the black overcheck on the green and one between the single tramlines.

BLUE	24		4		4					24	
BLACK		4		4		24			24		2
GREEN							24	24			
RED						6					6

MURRAY OF ELIBANK

BLUE	224			16		
BLACK		12		12		42
GREEN			48			
YELLOW						12

MURRAY OF TULLIBARDINE

This is said to have been adopted by Charles, first Earl of Dunmore, who was second son of the first Marquis of Tullibardine. It is recorded that in 1679 he was Lieutenant-Colonel of the Royal Grey Dragoons (later known as the Scots Greys).

BLUE	4		2		8		2			2		24				4	
RED		2		4		4		2	2		48		4		16	8	4
BLACK							4										2
GREEN													4	24			

NAPIER

A Lowland tartan in the Highland Society of London Collection, but it is not known when it was incorporated there. It features the stripe patterning associated with some MacDonald designs and has been called 'a Shepherd plaid blended with a true tartan'.

WHITE	2			4		8		4		4	
BLUE		24									
BLACK			8		4		4		4		8

NESBITT, NISBET

RED	10	56		6
WHITE		4		
BLACK			24	
GREEN				32

NITHSDALE

BLUE	20					
RED		4	12	2	2	12
GREEN			4	32	4	6

OGILVIE

Sett (a), the Ogilvie of Airlie, is the most complicated of all the tartan setts, and the most difficult to weave. One half of the mirror repeat of the sett, from one pivot point to the next, needs 862 threads, and as such would only fit into the 27-inch wide handwoven cloth if sett at 32 ends per inch. Originally known as Drummond of Strathallan, it obtained its present name in 1812, when the house of Ogilvie became connected by marriage. In sett (c), an earlier Ogilvie tartan, parts are so similar to that of sett (a) that it was thought by some to be an uncanny forecasting of the marriage alliance. Sett (b), the hunting tartan, is thought to be even older in origin, and legend has it that the fairies disliked the fact that this sett contained so much of their favourite colour — green — and cast spells against the clan during a battle, so that it lost to the enemy. It was then replaced by sett (c), which contained none of the offending colour.

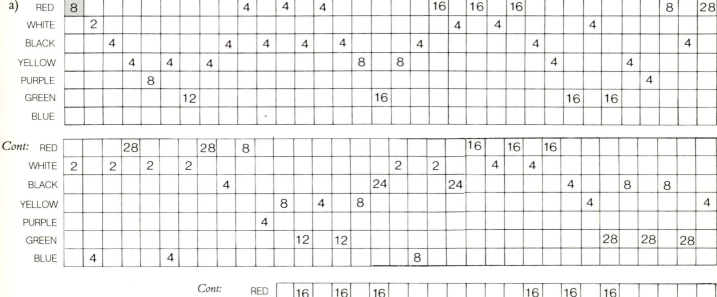

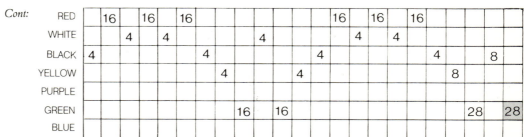

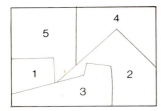

Photographs on pages 136 & 137
1. Morrison
2. Munro
3. Murray of Athol
4. Murray of Tullibardine
5. Napier

RED	**8**				
GREEN		6	6	32	
BLACK		2	2	16	
YELLOW					4
b) BLUE					**48**

WHITE	**4**			4	4	4		
LT. BLUE		10					20	**20**
YELLOW			4				10	
PURPLE			4					
c) RED				12	12	12		6

OLIPHANT
This sett was first recorded in the *Vestiarium Scoticum* and is rarely used now.

GREEN	4	64		
WHITE		2		
BLUE			48	**8**
BLACK			8	

RAMSAY
Various repressive laws, from 1563 to 1775, proscribed the name of the Clan MacGregor, and some members took the name of Ramsay at that time. The tartans are similar; sometimes the purple in this sett is interpreted as dark red.

RED	6	60		
PURPLE		2		
BLACK			56	**8**
WHITE			4	

RAMSAY, hunting
Also known as 'Blue Ramsay'.

BLUE	6	60		
BLACK		2	56	**8**
WHITE			4	

RATTRAY
This sett was first recorded in Johnson's book of 1906.

GREEN	142					
BLACK		8				
RED			8	8	72	
BLUE				18	8	8
WHITE						**8**

ROBERTSON

The Robertsons are known in Gaelic as Clan Donnachie. Sett (a) is the earliest of the Robertson tartans, with its characteristic white line, but sett (b) is more commonly used. Sett (c), the Robertson hunting, is reputed to have been in use before the 19th century. It is also known as Robertson of Kindeace.

a)
WHITE	2								2
GREEN		4			36			4	
RED			36	4	3	4	36		
BLUE				4		36	4		

b)
RED	2	18	2		2		2	18	2
GREEN			2		18			2	2
BLUE				2		18			

c)
WHITE	6										
BLACK		2	24	2		2	24	4		4	
BLUE			24					4	4		24
GREEN				32		32					
RED					6						

ROLLO

GREEN	30				30	30		30	
BLACK		30	4		30			30	
BLUE			30	30					
RED						6			
YELLOW									6

N.B. This sett is asymmetric.

ROSE, dress

This sett was described in the *Vestiarium Scoticum*.

GREEN	8					
RED		64				
PURPLE			18	4	4	
DK. RED				12	6	24
WHITE						6

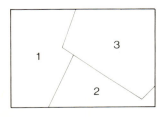

Photographs on pages 140 & 141
1. Ogilvie of Airlie
2. Ogilvie (hunting)
3. Ramsay (red) A.C.

ROSE, hunting

The hunting sett was known to have been is use in the early 19th century. (The tartan designed for the New York Fire Department Pipe Band was based on this one, with a light blue overcheck instead of red.)

BLACK	8		20		
WHITE		2			
GREEN			20		
BLUE				20	
RED					4

ROSS

Sett (a) is the traditional sett. Sett (b) is a modern hunting sett, based on a Ross sett in the *Vestiarium Scoticum*.

a)

GREEN	36	36	4	4									36	36
RED		4	36	8	36	4	36	2	2	36	2	2	36	4
BLUE					36	36		2	4	2	2	4	2		

b)

RED	2		2					
GREEN		4		24	4		6	2	4	4
BLACK					4	4			
LT. GREEN							2	2	8

RUSSELL

See Galbraith, Hunter, Mitchell.

RUTHVEN

A family tartan, shown originally in the *Vestiarium Scoticum*.

RED	4	60		
GREEN		2		30
BLUE			36	
WHITE				6

SCOTT

Sett (a) was described to Sir Walter Scott by Sir Thomas Dick Lauder, writing in 1829 about the publication of the *Vestiarium Scoticum*. The idea of Border families such as his having famous tartans was firmly repudiated by Sir Walter in his reply. In 1850, however, the black and white sett (b) was recorded, said to have been designed by Sir Walter for his own use, in private, as a Lowland shepherd's plaid.

a)

GREEN	8		28	8		8
RED		6	56	8		8
BLACK			2			
WHITE					6	

b)

WHITE	4	12		4		2	4	12
BLACK		2	12		2		2	12

SCRYMGEOUR

Designed by D. C. Stewart in 1970. The Earl of Dundee is Chief of this clan.

YELLOW	90		12	
BLACK		6		6
RED		12		90
BLUE		18		

SETON

A Lowland family tartan, recorded in the *Vestiarium Scoticum*.

RED	4		64	4		8		
GREEN		2					24	12
BLACK				8		8		
BLUE								
WHITE							2	

SHAW

This 'Green Shaw' is the most popular of the Shaw setts, and was illustrated in MacIain (1845). Shaws also wear the Mackintosh tartan.

GREEN	48				
BLACK		4	4		
BLUE			6	16	
RED					4

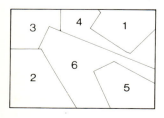

Photographs on pages 144 & 145
1. Robertson
2. Robertson (hunting)
3. Rose (dress) A.C.
4. Rose (hunting) A.C.
5. Ross
6. Ross (hunting)

SHAW OF TORDARROCH

A modern tartan, designed in 1966 by D. C. Stewart, for Major Shaw of Tordarroch, it is based on the Mackintosh structure to reflect that ancestry. It is also known as 'Red Shaw'. There is a hunting version in which the main area of red is changed to green.

LT. BLUE	10				
BLACK		2			
RED			60	16	16
PURPLE				30		4
GREEN					60

SINCLAIR

Sett (a) is the usual tartan, and it was recorded in the early 19th century. It is sometimes called the dress tartan. Sett (b), the hunting sett, was described in the *Vestiarium Scoticum*.

a)
RED	60			60
GREEN		24		
BLACK			10	
WHITE			4	
LT. BLUE				12

b)
GREEN	4	60			
RED		2			4
BLACK				32	
WHITE				2	
BLUE					32

SKENE

Although sett (a) is the tartan now associated with Skene, it was recorded under the name of 'Logan' many times, and was not called 'Skene' until the middle of the 19th century. Sett (b) was recorded in 1843 as 'Skene'.

a)
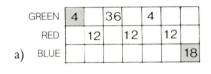

b)
BLACK	8		8		8		8		8		8
RED		6					6		
GREEN			48		48				
ORANGE				6					
BLUE									48

SMITH

This sett is also known as 'Hunting Gow'.

LT. BLUE	6			
BLUE		36		
BLACK			40	2
GREEN			40	
YELLOW				6

SOMERVILLE

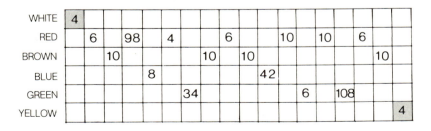

147

STEWART OF APPIN
This sett is thought to be of some antiquity.

GREEN	4			4		4	48			
RED		4	48	4	4	8		4		6
LT. BLUE		2							2	
BLUE			4		16				4	

STEWART OF ATHOL
This sett is thought to have derived from a relic of the '45. It appears in the manuscript version of the *Vestiarium Scoticum* (1829).

RED	12	40				
BLACK		2	16	2	2	
GREEN				6	4	44

STEWART, black
As Royal Stewart, but with black ground instead of red. Designed by the trade.

STUART OF BUTE

WHITE	4						
RED		48					24
BLACK			12	2	2		
GREEN				2	4	12	

STEWART, dress (Victoria)

RED	4						8	4	
WHITE		48	6		2				2
LT. BLUE			6						
BLACK				12	2	2		2	
YELLOW				2					
GREEN							16		

STEWART, FINGASK
A thread count taken from the cloak worn by Prince Charles Edward now at Fingask Castle.

RED	96		16			
BLUE		6		6		
YELLOW		2				
GREEN			28			
LT. BLUE					8	
WHITE						2

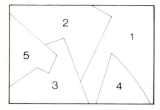

Photographs on pages 148 & 149
1. Scott
2. Seton
3. Shaw A.C.
4. Sinclair
5. Skene

STUART OF GALLOWAY
This sett was prepared for, but not used in, the *Vestiarium Scoticum,* and was not otherwise recorded until the end of the 19th century, after which it became popular.

BLACK	6	8	4			2		
RED		48					6	4
YELLOW			2					
WHITE					2			2
BLUE					8			
GREEN						12		

STEWART, hunting
A very popular design, worn widely by those who have no specific tartan. It appears in the Wilson Pattern Book of 1819.

GREEN	4				24	24	4	4
BLUE		6	2	2				
BLACK			2	2	8		6	12
RED / YELLOW						4		

STEWART, old or ancient
Although there are many setts for this tartan, this one is the most used today. It is said by some to originate from the Stewarts of the Western Highlands, and became accepted as the Clan Stewart tartan.

GREEN	24			24				4	4	
BLACK		2	2		24	24		2	2	2
BLUE			4				24			24
RED					4	2	4			

STUART, Royal

RED	72						8	4
LT. BLUE		8						
BLACK			12	2	2		2	
YELLOW				2				
WHITE						2		2
GREEN						16		

STRATHEARN

This sett was evolved for King George VI (also Earl of Strathearn). Although the name of a district, it is not a district tartan.

YELLOW	2		16			16		2			2
RED		2		2	2		12		12	2	
GREEN		12			2			2	2	12	

SUTHERLAND

See Regimental Tartans page 164.

BLUE	22		2		2				16	2
BLACK		2		2		16	2	16		2
GREEN						16	16			

GREEN	12		48						
WHITE		4							
BLACK				24	4	4			
BLUE				6		4	24	2	
RED								2	6

TAYLOR

GREEN	16		26	24	10	
BLACK		4				
CORAL PINK			8			
PURPLE					44	
YELLOW						6

THOMSON

See MacTavish.

URQUHART

This sett was collected in the Highlands before 1822, almost certainly by George Hunter, an army clothier, who was touring the Highlands in search of clan tartans for the George IV visit to Edinburgh. Another version, similar to the Black Watch, is recorded in the *Vestiarium Scoticum*. (The author of the ancient manuscript on which that was based was 'Sir Richard Urquhart'.)

BLACK	4		12		2		2		
GREEN		18							
BLUE					2		2	12	
RED									6

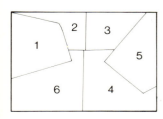

Photographs on pages 152 & 153
1. Stewart of Appin
2. Stewart of Athol A.C.
3. Stuart of Bute
4. Stewart, Fingask
5. Hunting Stewart
6. Old, or Ancient, Stewart A.C.

WAGGRALL

One of the most complicated tartan setts (see also Ogilvie of Airlie). It appears in the Wilson Pattern Book of 1819.

ROSE	8		4																						4
WHITE		2		4		4		4		2		2		4		4		4		2		4			
RED			22																						22
PURPLE					22			22					10							12		12			
LT. BLUE						8		8										4				4			
LT. GREEN									8					8		8		8							
YELLOW										8		8													
GREEN															20		20								

Continued:

ROSE		8		4									4		8
WHITE	2		2		4		2		4		2		4		2
RED		22												22	
PURPLE					12	12									
LT. BLUE				4		4									
LT. GREEN							4		4						
YELLOW								4	4						
GREEN							12				12				

WALLACE

This sett was recorded in the *Vestiarium Scoticum,* and is thought to be one of the earliest authenticated tartans. Wallaces also wear MacLean of Duart.

BLACK	2		16	
RED		16		
YELLOW				2

WATSON

BLUE	48		4		4			
BLACK		4				40		
RED			4					
GREEN					32		4	
YELLOW							4	6

WELLINGTON

BLACK	8				
LT. BLUE		6			
BLUE			22		
GREEN				28	
WHITE					4

WEMYSS

The tartan of a Fifeshire family, first shown in the *Vestiarium Scoticum.*

RED	8		48	8			8
GREEN		2					
BLACK				8	24	24	
WHITE						2	

WILSON

BLUE	60	6		6		6							8		
WHITE			4											4	
GREEN				6	6		32	6		6		6		50	8
RED						6			6		6		6		30		16	30

TARTANS OF THE ROYAL FAMILY

Tartans – and Highland dress – are inextricably linked with the fortunes of the Kings and Queens of Scotland and England. Indeed, it could be argued that the fall of the House of Stewart, and the failure of the Jacobite uprisings, which in turn led to the Proscription of 1746, almost put an end to the tartan; and that had it not been maintained as part of the military uniform (see pages 164-171), both the tartan and Highland dress might have disappeared forever. On the other hand it was the renewed interest in tartans and Highland dress taken by the Hanoverian court at the end of the 18th century, culminating in George IV's visit to Edinburgh in 1822, that did much to revive tartans and the wearing of the Highland dress – an interest that was continued and enhanced by Queen Victoria (see page 29) and has been maintained by the Royal Family ever since.

Tartans have been the subject of myths and legends throughout their history, and this characteristic continues in the 20th century. According to Lord Lyon King of Arms there are only two royal tartans: Royal Stewart and Balmoral. Yet when it comes to what tartans the Royals actually wear, the choice is considerably wider. Prince Charles, for example, has made it clear that only he is entitled to wear the Duke of Rothesay tartan — which relates to one of his Scottish titles — and the same must also be true of the MacDonald, Lord of the Isles tartan, since *that* title was annexed to the Scottish Crown by James IV in 1493. Yet the latter is in fact woven commercially: if worn by Prince Charles, it would almost certainly be in a version woven to his own specification.

In the history of the tartan, it has already been suggested (page 10) that the number of colours woven into a tartan denoted rank, with the King or *Ard-righ* using seven (and only officiating clergy wearing eight!). Certainly, there are records quoted by Frank Adam in *The Clans, Septs and Highland Regiments of the Scottish Highlands* suggesting that this was so in Western Scotland as late as the 15th century, though the cost of weaving more variegated tartans may have been as important a factor as their symbolic significance. It is known that James III of Scotland's bed had drapes and curtains of 'variand purpur tartar, bowdin with thissilis and a unicorn' in 1488, and that the very first mention of tartan in trade is found in an account tendered to the same King's Treasurer in 1471 for 'four elne and ane halve of tartane for a . . . price an elne 10s, £2.5s'. We also know (see page 13) of the references to tartan ordered for King James V for his Highland progress in 1538.

When it comes to royal tartans which have either a history that goes back to the Proscription or before – or royal tartans of a much more recent date – one of the oldest is the Royal Stewart, which some believe belongs to the Royal House of Scotland rather than the Royal House of Stewart. Whatever the case may be, the tartan was described by George V as 'my personal tartan' and its design certainly echoes the ribbons worn by Charles II at his coronation in 1660. In a white sett, it is worn by ladies of the Royal Family. This version is thought to have been designed by Prince Albert and is called Victoria after his queen.

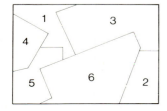

Photographs on pages 156 & 157
1. Strathearn
2. Sutherland
3. Urquhart
4. Wallace
5. Wallace (hunting)
6. Wemyss

Photograph showing the four sons of King George V: the Duke of Kent, the Duke of Windsor in Highland dress, George VI and the Duke of Gloucester.

Left, a print of Queen Victoria and her children in Royal Stewart tartan by John Calcott Horsley and, top right, two royal tartans. On top is the Balmoral Tartan, which was registered by Edward VIII, the copyright being held by Her Majesty the Queen who grants permission as to who may wear it. Underneath is the Royal Stewart, which is also classed as a royal tartan by Lord Lyon. Nevertheless, it is one of the most popular bought by the public, often in the belief that anyone (including the English) who owes allegiance to the British Crown is entitled to wear it. Below, a photograph by Patrick Lichfield of Prince Charles, aged 24, playing with his cousin, Lady Sarah Armstrong-Jones, at Balmoral. The Prince's kilt is in the Balmoral tartan.

There are in fact many variations of the Royal Stewart tartan, including the dark setting which is now known as the Black Watch (and which began life as the Government or Universal sett, see page 167). There are also versions of the Black Watch tartan itself which are used for other Regiments, for example, a Black Watch tartan in lighter shades is used for the Argyll and Sutherland Highlanders, and the Black Watch with a yellow overcheck for the Gordon Highlanders.

Similarly, the Royal Stewart tartan itself is worn by the pipers in the Black Watch, the King's Own Scottish Borderers, the Royal Scots and the Scots Guards, though the *soldiers* in some of these regiments actually wear other tartans: the King's Own Scottish Borderers wear the Leslie tartan, and the Royal Scots wear Hunting Stewart trews (and the 7/9 (Territorial Army) Battalion Hunting Stewart kilts). The Scots Guards do not wear tartan at all.

Apart from the Royal Stewart tartan in all its variations and the Balmoral tartan which is exclusively reserved for the Royal Family (see page 29), there are, as already mentioned, tartans which relate to titles held by the Royal Family. These include not only the Lord of the Isles and Duke of Rothesay, but also the Strathearn, which was originally made for George IV who was Earl of Strathearn and is an example of a tartan named after a district which is not a district tartan; the Inverness, which was worn in 1829 by the Earl of Inverness and was worn (with a slightly different sett) by George V when he was the Duke of York and Earl of Inverness, and later, in 1930, by George VI when *he* was Earl of Inverness; and the St Andrews tartan, which belongs to the Earl of St Andrews (the son of the Duke of Kent). There are also other tartans, like the Princess Louise, that were commissioned specially for a royal personage. In addition to these tartans with direct links to the Royal Family, there are several that retain direct connections with Prince Charles Edward. These include the tartan that bears his name and others, like a sett of Drummond of Perth, which relates to a cloak worn by the Prince which he left at Fingask Castle near Perth before leaving Scotland in 1746, and the MacDonald of Kingsburgh whose sett was taken from the fragment of a waistcoat given to the Prince by Alexander MacDonald of Kingsburgh after the defeat at Culloden. A connection with the Prince is also preserved in the MacDonald of Keppoch tartan whose sett is based on a plaid given to the Prince by The Keppoch in 1745.

This method of recording royal connections also applies to one sett of the MacDuff tartan which is similar to the Royal Stewart (commemorating links between the Earls of Fife and the Crown); and the Maitland, which was designed in 1953 for the standard bearers in Queen Elizabeth's II's Coronation procession. It is one of the few tartans protected by a patent. But, just as a tartan can acquire royal associations, so it can also lose them: the MacLaren was originally called the Regent until the Prince Regent became George IV in 1820, when the tartan acquired its current name.

Fact and fiction surround royal tartans juast as they do many others; the MacBeth tartan could even be regarded as a royal one since MacBethad MacFinlaeg was a Celtic king of Scotland from 1040-1057. It is in fact a version of the Royal Stewart, but with a blue ground instead of a red one, and it is probable that the name 'MacBeth' was attached to this design when it was realized that the sett had royal connections. Royalty, like the clans, serve their particular purpose and the tartan is richer for it.

PHOTOGRAPH BY PATRICK LICHFIELD OF THE QUEEN SURROUNDED BY BLACK LABRADORS IN THE GARDEN AT BALMORAL. THE QUEEN IS WEARING THE BALMORAL TARTAN.

REGIMENTAL TARTANS

> A mottled garment with numerous colours hanging in folds to the calf of the leg, with a girdle round the loins over the garment.

Thus did an Irishman vividly describe the dress of Scottish auxiliaries despatched to Ireland in 1594.

From written evidence such as this, beginning with descriptions of the Gaelic tribes at the time of the Roman Empire, and Scottish warriors en route for the Holy Land during the Crusades, from effigies in stone, and from illustrated manuscripts, it is possible to picture the appearance of Scottish fighting men over the centuries. Daniel Defoe, in his *Memories of a Cavalier,* wrote of Scottish soldiers in 1639 that

> Their dress was an antique as the rest (of their equipment): a cap on their heads called a bonnet, long hanging sleeves behind, and their doublet-breeches of a stuff they called plaid, striped across red and yellow, with short cloaks of the same.

Surprisingly enough, the very first regiment of the British Army was Scottish. This was the 1st of Foot, later the Royal Scots Regiment, which was originally raised by the King of France to fight in France in 1633 but which, following the Restoration

BELOW, 'ALMA: FORWARD THE 42ND' BY R. GIBB. IT WAS THIS REGIMENT THAT BECAME KNOWN AS THE BLACK WATCH, GIVING ITS NAME TO THE TARTAN. RIGHT, HUGH, 12TH EARL OF EGLINTON, WEARING THE UNIFORM OF THE BLACK WATCH, FROM A PAINTING BY COPLEY.

of King Charles II in 1660, was taken on to the British establishment in 1661. Little is known of what these soldiers wore, except that they were dressed in a uniform that was a simplified version of the clothing worn by gentlemen of fashion (who provided the commissioned officers). By this time, as W. A. Thorburn points out in his article *Military Origins of Scottish National Dress*,

> ... the land forces of the major European nations could be immediately recognized by the colour and cut of their clothing, and elaborate combinations of lace, facing colour, headdress and even shape of cuffs, which distinguished the many different regiments and military functions.

But there were no formalized Highland or Scottish military dress. Scottish soldiers in the British Army would have worn the same uniform as all the other soldiers, the only differences being the colour of their facings.

Thus, at the beginning of the 18th century, those Scots who had enlisted in the British Army wore the army uniform of the day, while those Scots who owed allegiance to Highland Chiefs in rebellion against the House of Hanover wore a form of Highland dress that was extemely fluid and could lead to horrendous problems. Even at Culloden, as a Highland officer noted (see page 19), the MacDonalds found it very difficult to distinguish one branch of the clan from another, despite the fact that they were fighting on opposite sides of the battle.

Curiously enough, given the extreme unease with which the more remote parts of Scotland were regarded by the British Government in London, a form of Highland military dress did emerge before Culloden. In 1725, six independent companies of soldiers were raised in the Highlands, and in 1739 they were formed into a regiment, first numbered as the 43rd and later called the 42nd, the Royal Highland Regiment. This regiment is better known as the Black Watch (a watch being originally a guard mounted against cattle rustlers, hence the word 'blackguard'), and all subsequent units raised in the Highlands wore the same uniform, although they were distinguished by different facing colours and increasingly varied (and variable!) regimental details. The soldiers were dressed in a belted plaid with a British Army red coat, cut shorter to accommodate the plaid, and were allowed to carry broadswords and pistols in addition to the standard infantry equipment.

PAINTING OF THE ROYAL NORTH BRITISH DRAGOONS AND
92ND HIGHLANDERS BY J.G.P. FISCHER.

Just which tartans were worn by the Independent Companies raised in 1725 seems open to doubt, but there is little question that the Highland Regiment of 1739 wore the dark tartan now known as the Black Watch. This became available to all Government regiments as the Government or Universal Sett, and thus the official tartan of the day – a tartan which, incidentally, had no regional or family associations. But it must also be remembered that, as there was no indenting to central stores in the 18th century, the weaving of the tartan would have been done by different people in different places, so that even the Government or Universal Sett could have varied considerably in quality and even in design. However, its authorization did mean that, perhaps for the first time in history, a substantial number of people were clothed in a Highland costume of uniform appearance, with a regulated tartan and identical accessories.

The raising of the Black Watch was followed by Louden's Highlanders and then, following the Proscription of 1746 (which incidentally banned not only the wearing of Highland dress, but also the playing of the bagpipes), only the Highland Regiments in the King's service continued to wear a form of Highland military dress that maintained a tradition established before the '45 rebellion. Indeed, it could be argued that had the military dress not survived, and had there not been a Celtic Revival south of the Border at the same time, nothing would be left of the Highland dress today. And, as new regiments were formed, so the Black Watch tartan was modified: in 1778, for example, the 73rd (later the 71st) Regiment of Highlanders was raised by John Mackenzie, Lord MacLeod, who added buff and red lines to the Black Watch tartan to give it a regimental distinction. Later, the buff lines were changed to white, making the tartan the same as worn by the 78th, another Mackenzie regiment, and it is this tartan that was worn by the Highland Light Infantry and the Seaforth Highlanders in more recent times.

Another example of modifications being made to the Black Watch tartan is the Gordon, which is the same but has an additional line in the yellow regimental facing colour. It was added after the 4th Duke of Gordon, who raised the regiment, asked his supplier, Forsyth of Huntly, to provide a distinctive tartan for his soldiers, and Forsyth thought that a yellow line would look 'very lively'. As the Gordon family had no tartan, the regimental tartan has also become the clan tartan.

GERMAN WOODUCT SHOWING SOLDIERS OF MACKAY'S REGIMENT ARRIVING IN STETTIN IN 1630

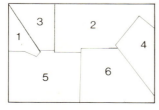

Photographs on pages 168 & 169
1. Argyll & Sutherland Highlanders
2. Atholl Highlanders
3. Black Watch
4. Erracht Cameron Q.O.H.
5. Hunting Stewart Royal Scots
6. Red Gordon

Such *ad hoc* variations are, in fact, typical: choosing a tartan for the Cameron Highlanders, for example, proved difficult because neither the Cameron nor Keppoch tartans, which were predominantly red, looked well against the British Army red coats. Legend has it that Mrs Cameron of Erracht suggested that by blending the yellow lines of the Cameron tartan with the green lines of the Clan McDonald, a satisfactory design would emerge. Certainly, the Cameron Highlanders was the only Scottish Regiment that had a tartan specially designed for it.

While the marrying of Scottish tartans with the British Army red coat was one obvious (and radical) change to the Highland dress, another was the adoption of the *philabeg* or small kilt which also predates the '45 Rebellion. The reasons for the emergence of the small kilt among the civilian population have already been discussed (see pages 20-23), and in the army one reason for adopting the small kilt may have been that it cost less to provide than the full plaid. But there is also evidence that when Highland troops began fighting in the virgin forests of North America — as opposed to the relatively open landscape of Europe — the plaid became an encumbrance, whereas the small kilt was more suited to the new terrain and much easier to replace. (It was a change of climate and geography which probably led to the kilt being replaced by tartan trousers in India.) The kilt was then pleated to gather in the cloth in a neat and tidy fashion, while the 'top half' of the kilt became an ornamental but rather useless plaid. The sporran became more and more elaborate, not to say bizarre, and the flat blue bonnet of the Highlander was transformed into a strange form of military headgear increasingly adorned by feathers and plumes, becoming by the late 19th century an elaborate wire cage. In the 18th century the bonnets were adorned in North America by turkey feathers or bear fur, and elsewhere by ostrich feathers. When the Highlanders fought in the Crimean War (1853-1856), they looked quite unlike any other soldiers in the world!

Following the Crimean War, a change was made to the traditional red coat, which was cut down in size to become a doublet that allowed the kilt to be free all around and the sporran to hang down freely. But the evolution of this increasingly fanciful and flamboyant military dress did not proceed unchallenged. In April 1809, for instance, six Highland regiments had to discard their Highland uniforms in favour of that of the ordinary infantry, largely because these particular regiments no longer contained a high proportion of Scottish Highlanders but men from other parts of Britain who had no desire to wear what they considered outlandish clothing. The Celtic Revival of the 1820s (see pages 24-29) did something to reverse this trend, and in 1824 the first of these six regiments reverted to wearing Highland dress, though changing from the kilt to the trews. Trews, or perhaps more accurately 'tartan trousers', were adopted by another three Highland regiments later in the century. And, just as Queen Victoria had had a tremendous influence on the revival of the tartan (see page 29), so she also influenced its use in military uniform, changing kilts worn by ordinary ranks from being made out of a hard wool to being made from a softer wool:

> In the autumn of 1872, Her Majesty having noted that a detachment of the 93rd (the Guard of Honour at Ballater) wore kilts and plaids of hard tartan, and that after a march in wind and rain the men's knees were much scratched and cut by the sharp edge of the tartan, the Queen was graciously pleased to direct that soft instead of hard tartan be in future supplied to Highland regiments.

The next major change to Highland uniforms came in 1881, when it was decided that all Lowland infantry would also wear Highland dress — a decision that pleased neither the Highland regiments, whose identity was thus watered down, nor the Lowland regiments, who considered the change an insult to their own historical identity and their seniority, since they predated the Highland Regiments by one hundred years or more. The result was to turn Scotland, at least from a military point of view, into a tartan nation. Thus tartan trousers and Highland doublets were issued instead of the infantry uniform then in use to all but, amazingly, the *Scots* Guards, who refused to be put into tartan. Writing in *Lowland Scots Regiments* which was published in 1918 (but compiled before the First World War), its editor, Sir Herbert Maxwell, who was Hon. Lt. Colonel of the 3rd Royal Scots Fusiliers, said:

> The uniform of the Lowland Scots Infantry at the present day cannot be deemed satisfactory either in an historic or aesthetic sense . . . Tartan trews are not one whit more appropriate to Lowland infantry than would be the philabeg and sporran, but here they are, and the course seems to be to carry the change, acknowledging the Highland dress as a national military costume. Tartan is not essential, nor the theatrical feather bonnet.

The changeover in dress that affected the Lowland regiments also affected Volunteer and Territorial units raised between 1859-1914 which gradually adopted the Highland or semi-Highland uniforms of their parent formations.

But, just as the enthusiasm for clan tartans earlier in the 19th century led to a lot of new (or spuriously authenticated) designs, so completely new regimental tartans appeared at the end of the century – at a time, in fact, when the formal set-battle was giving way to a different kind of warfare, a warfare in which discreet manoeuvres and surprise attack were becoming important. Thus, in the South African war at the turn of the century, Highland regiments wore for the first time a small khaki apron over the front of their kilts to act as camouflage, and at the beginning of the First World War, their apron was extended to conceal the whole kilt. Besides being affected by changes in tactics in warfare the kilt was also affected by changes in weapons, most notably by the use of mustard gas against which it gave little protection. Nevertheless, the kilt continued to be used in battle until the evacuation of the British Army from Dunkirk in 1940, though there were instances later in the Second World War when it was seen, a memorable occasion being when it was worn by the massed pipes and drums of the 51st Highland Division as they marched into Tripoli in 1944.

Today, neither the kilt nor trews are worn on active service. During and after the Second World War, bonnets were worn and Scottish soldiers also had small tartan patches on their battle dress, but since that has now been replaced by combat jackets, only the bonnets with their Regimental badges remain. Hence it is left to the pipe and military bands to maintain the splendour of the Highland military uniforms which, as W. A. Thorburn points out,

> have nothing to do with any long Scottish traditions as such, but are in every detail an emotional sight and sound evolved as part of the British Army over the last one hundred years. Like nearly all of the continued Scottish ceremonials with a Highland flavour, they owe their existence not so much to folk tradition but to factors connected with the United Kindom Establishment. Although Prince Charles Edward Stuart is part of the legend, he took no conscious part in its development, but George IV and Queen Victoria did a great deal to create and sustain all that patriotic Scots now believe to be their own.

DISTRICT TARTANS

The evolution of clan tartans, and the myths surrounding their history, have already been described; and because most clan tartans are 19th and 20th century inventions, the case for district tartans predating them seems very plausible. As J. Telfer Dunbar has written:

> The origin of tartan was probably first one of association with a region. Early travellers tell us that a person's place of origin could be told from his tartan rather than his name. This stood to reason since in early times, most people did not use family names. Neighbours used the same weavers and dyestuffs to produce their clothing. Traces of this can be seen even in modern tartans where the majority of older clans from the west are blue-green based: MacLeod, MacDonald, Campbell, MacNeil and MacLean. Many of those from the north are also variations of wide darker stripes on a red ground. The Mackintosh, Robertson, Grant and MacGillivray are all variations on this theme. Therefore, the concept of 'district' tartan is older than that of 'clan' tartan. It was a natural transition from the 'district' to association with a prominent family of the area. Today, individuals having no tartan associated with their particular name should take pride in the 'district' tartan associated with their family or alternatively, an area of Scotland that they have visited and enjoyed.

However, plausible though this argument may seem, there are in fact very few district tartans that go back before the '45 Rebellion, and the list of district tartans given by Mr Dunbar — originally 54, to which another five could be added — contains only four that fit the description of early tartans clearly defining a person's geographical origin. These are the Huntly, Loch Laggan, Perth and the Glen Orchy. The Huntly tartan was popular in the 18th century, when it was worn by members of the Brodie, Forbes and Gordon families, who were Jacobites, though it was originally the tartan of Clan Macrae. The Glen Orchy tartan is probably the best-authenticated district tartan there is, since the MacIntyres of Glen Orchy were weavers who worked in the area from the 15th to the 19th century, during which time they established a local tradition of weaving that could be clearly identified.

The main impulse for district tartans, however, came from Wilsons of Bannockburn who, as described on pages 23-24, scoured Scotland in search of tartan designs to meet the demand for them at the end of the 18th century and the beginning of the 19th. Thus, among Mr Dunbar's list of 'district' tartans, there are many that originate from this source, including Aberdeen (one of many popular 'town setts'), Arran, Blair Logie, Crieff, Dundee, Fort William, Gala Water, Glen Lyon, Glasgow, Leith, Lenzie and Mull.

There are also many other 'district' tartans which should more properly be described as 'trade setts'. Among these are Angus, Applecross, Carrick, Clanedin, Edinburgh, Deeside, Galloway, Inverary, Largs, Moffat, Musselburgh, Nithsdale, Paisley, Roxburgh, Strathclyde and Tweedside. Quite a number, of which Roxburgh is an example, go back to the 19th century. Others, like Garrick, Galloway and Nithsdale, were first produced in the 1930s; while a few, like Strathclyde, are very recent.

Besides the Wilson 'district' tartans and trade setts, there are number of tartans belonging to families that have a clearly-defined territorial base so that it could be argued that these tartans (as suggested by J. Telfer Dunbar) have a district (regional) significance too. Among them are Argyll, Buchan, Cunningham, Dunbar, Eglinton, Mar, Monteith, Nairn and Renwick. There are also a few borderline cases, like Drumlithie, which is both a family and a Wilson tartan; and others, like Dunblane and Lennox, where the authority for the design seems to have originated from a family portrait. In the case of the Lennox tartan, although this sett was worn by the Countess of Lennox who was the mother of Henry Darnley (the second husband of Mary Stuart) in a 16th-century portrait, it is shaky evidence on which to base a 'district' tartan since the tartan could have been Douglas (the Countess was Lady Margaret Douglas), Stewart (she was the wife of Matthew Stewart), or Angus (her father was the Earl of Angus).

What are sometimes described as 'district' tartans also includes some that are royal. Among these are Inverness, Rothesay, St Andrews and Strathearn (the last designed for the Earl of Strathearn who was the father of Queen Victoria), and Duke of Fife, which is a trade sett named after a royal personage. And there are others that are 'military', including Strathspey and Sutherland. There is also one 'district' tartan that is an odd-man-out: Culloden, which is based on a piece of cloth picked up from the battlefield in 1746.

Finally, there is one 'district' tartan that belongs to a Highland Society, the Stirling & Bannockburn, and one that is simply wrong – the Border tartan. This is derived from the special design woven around the edges of a plaid and has nothing whatever to do with the geographical region of that name.

THE DISTRICT TARTAN 'LENNOX'

FOREIGN TARTANS

Scotland is connected to other countries by innumerable family ties, the result of the travels and emigration of countless Scotsmen and women: soldiers, merchants, engineers, missionaries, doctors and their families. They took the tartan with them. There are tartans woven for women's dresses in Sarna in Norway which are probably derived from tartans worn by Scottish soldiers who fought in Sinclair's expedition to Norway in 1738-40; there is also a Dutch tartan which is a Mackay tartan woven in the colours of the Dutch flag which goes back to the 300 Scottish soldiers who fought in the Netherlands under the Chief of Mackay for Gustavus Adolphus in 1631; and there is a tartan worn in a Portuguese fishing village today that is said to be derived from the tartans worn by Scottish soldiers in the Peninsular War.

Other Scottish tartans with overseas connections that have military origins include the MacLean tartan streamers worn by the Royal pipe band in Morocco, which commemorate the days when General Caid Sir Harry MacLean restored the army in that country, and the Childers tartan worn by the Ghurka battalions. On the Indian sub-continent, there are also tartans in Pakistan and Bangladesh that are believed to stem from tartans worn by Scots serving with the East India Company in the 18th century, while further east in Malaysia, the Sultan of Johore has a tartan given to him by Queen Victoria. Other potentates to possess tartans of their own include Sultan Oman Stuart Quaboos of the Oman and Sheikh Makhtoum of Dubai.

However, widespread though these tartans are, none (except the Johore and Ghurka tartans) has any official standing (in Scottish terms, that is). Only in Canada has some attempt been made to give a number of tartans a seal of official approval – a move that began in 1880 when Canadian weavers published their *Clan Originaux* collection of *Irish* tartans for clans like the Connors, Murphys and O'Keefes, which were in fact based on Scottish tartans. Perhaps because of this, the previous Lord Lyon King of Arms, Sir Thomas Innes of Learney, decided to put some order into the situation by recording the tartans of the Canadian Provinces, when they were submitted to him by the Governors. These tartans were recorded at the Court of the Lord Lyon in New Register House, Edinburgh. (Canada, incidentally, has produced an Olympic tartan, with the five interlocking Olympic rings appliqued over every alternate square in the sett.)

Just as Canada has many links with Scotland through both the influx of Scottish emigrants and their continuing use of the tartan, so these links can also be found in the United States. The Georgia tartan, for example, relates to the founding of the State which, as Dr Micheil MacDonald, Director of the Scottish Tartans Society has noted, goes back to June 1732 when:

> King George II gave a Charter to a 'Jacobite' English Squire James Oglethorpe, and twenty other 'Trustees', to establish a new American colony. The colony would be named 'GEORGIA' after the King. Oglethorpe landed at Savannah on February 12th 1733 with 112 settlers, and in the early years of the settlement, came to rely heavily on a band of Highlanders from Inverness-shire, led by the redoubtable John Mor McIntosh, direct descendant of the sixteenth Chief of the Clan Mackintosh. In concert

with the Creek Indians, whose Chiefs – by an early intermarriage – bear the proud name MacIntosh to this day, those Highlanders were responsible for preventing a Spanish invasion from Florida and Cuba. Without them, the whole of North America might well be a Spanish possession now; a fact which would have dramatically changed the world we live in!

As a result of this connection, Dr MacDonald notes, the Georgia tartan reflects elements in Scottish history which also have a bearing upon the State of Georgia. The sett incorporates the red and azure motif from the royal tartan of the time of George II, based on a specimen from a jacket of the Royal Company of Archers (the personal bodyguard to the Sovereign in Scotland) of the 1730s. The underlying pattern of the sett incorporates the colours of the earliest known Mackintosh tartan while the blacks and greens of the Georgia sett relate to the tartan worn by the Independent Highland Company of Foot raised by Captain McIntosh under the orders of James Oglethorpe in 1740 – basically the Government or Universal sett (see page 167). Thus the Georgia tartan, which the State sponsored in 1981, is an excellent example of how historical and geographical associations can be designed into a sett, giving a piece of cloth a symbolism far beyond what anyone would normally expect.

WATERCOLOURS BY A.E. HASWELL MILLER SHOWING THE INFLUENCE OF SCOTTISH MILITARY DRESS ON CANADIAN AND NEW ZEALAND TROOPS IN THE MANITOBA AND QUEBEC REGIMENTS AND THE 14TH INFANTRY BATTALION

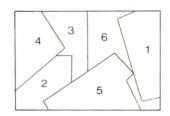

Photographs on pages 176 & 177
1. Georgia
2. Johore
3. Maple Leaf
4. North West Territory
5. Nova Scotia
6. U.S.A. Bi-Centennial

LORD LYON KING OF ARMS

No herald in Europe exercised such powers of prerogative, was vested with such high dignity, or possessed so high a rank. In his armorial jurisdiction, Lyon stands in place of The King.

Lord Lyon Depute Boswell, 1796 (Lyon's Office Records)

Lord Lyon King of Arms is one of Scotland's great Officers of State who plays a role in Scotland which is similar to that undertaken by the Earl Marshal (the hereditary office of the Dukes of Norfolk) in England, where he is responsible for organising the pageantry of royal weddings, coronations and funerals, for example. However, unlike the Earl Marshal, Lord Lyon is also a member of the Royal Household. The role played by Lord Lyon in the preparation, conduct and record of state and royal ceremonial incorporates the pre-heraldic Celtic office of High Sennachie of the Royal Line of Scotland, and in this capacity as guardian and preserver of the Royal Pedigree and Family Records, the Lord Lyon's certificate was required for the coronation of each Scottish king. Lord Lyon is responsible for the whole of the Crown's prerogative in armorial matters: today this responsibility is exercised over the granting of a coat of arms, and a Royal Warrant does not become effective until presented in Lyon Court. The tartans that are incorporated in a coat of arms are those that are recorded in the Public Register of All Arms and Bearings and it is in determining the right to the undifferenced Arms and thus the Headship of clans or Chieftainship of families that Lord Lyon recognises a number of Chiefs, and thus their right to determine their clan tartans.

It was the previous Lord Lyon, Sir Thomas Innes of Learney, who decided to establish a record of those tartans determined by the Clan Chiefs, beginning with Forbes (ancient) and Mackenzie. The record now includes Agnew, Arbuthnot, Boyd, Cameron, Clan Chattan, Chief of Clan Chattan, Cochrane, Davidson, Farquharson, Gayre (dress), Grant, Gunn, Hogarth of Firhill, Innes, Innes (hunting), Jardine, Kincaid of Kincaid, Leask, McBain, MacDonald of Clanranald (dress and hunting), McFarlane, MacInnes, MacIntyre, McKerrell of Hillhouse (hunting), MacKinnon (clan and hunting), Mackintosh (dress and hunting), MacThomas, Maitland, Mar Tribe, Moncrieffe, Morrison Clan, Rattray, Rose, Shaw of Tordarroch, Sinclair and Thomson. As can be seen, it is by no means a comprehensive list since it is entirely up to the Chiefs whether they submit their tartans to Lord Lyon or not. Furthermore, each tartan has to be considered by his Tartans Advisory Commitee, which includes representatives from Scottish woollen manufacturers, before approval is given. This is a lengthy process, taking two years or more, and only some three to four tartans are currently being considered every year.

A particular privilege of the Lord Lyon lies in his role as recorder of Canadian tartans, which began with that of Nova Scotia in 1956. The Canadian tartans now recorded in the Lyon Court Books include British Columbia, Bruce County, Manitoba, New Brunswick, Newfoundland and Saskatchewan, with a tartan for the Yukon Territory currently under consideration. Some of these tartans have also been incorporated into the laws passed by the Canadian Provincial legislatures, and so have a legal status there. Here again we have an example of the universal role of the tartan as a bond between nations.

Lord Lyon King of Arms flanked by Unicorn Pursuivant (now the Islay Herald) and Carrick Pursuivant photographed on Lord Lyon's inauguration in 1981.

THE MAIN HIGHLAND CLANS

BUCHANAN
CAMERON (MACGRILLONIE, MACMARTIN)
CAMPBELL (MACARTHUR, MACPHUN)
CLAN CHATTAN
CHISHOLM
COLQUHOUN
CUMMING
CLAN DONALD
DRUMMOND
ERSKINE
FARQUHARSON
FERGUSSON
FORBES
FRASER
GALBRAITH
GORDON
GRAHAM
GRANT
GUNN
HAMILTON
HAY
INNES
LAMONT
LINDSAY
LIVINGSTONE (MACLEAY)
MACALISTER
MACAULAY
MACCALLUM
MACDONNELL
MACDOUGAL
CLAN MACDUFF
MACEWEN
MACFARLANE
MACFIE

MACGREGOR
MACKAY
MACKENZIE (MATHESON, MACRAE)
MACKINNON
MACKINTOSH (FARQUHARSON, SHAW)
MACLACHLAN
MACLAREN
MACLEAN
MACLEOD
MACMILLAN
MACNAB (DEWAR)
MACNACHTAN
MACNEIL
MACPHERSON
MACQUARIE
MACQUEEN
McCORQUODALE
MENZIES
MONCREIFFE
MORRISON
MUNRO
MURRAY (MORAY, BUTTER, ATHOLL HIGHLANDERS)
OGILVY
OLIPHANT
CLAN RANALD
RATTRAY
ROBERTSON (DUNCAN, REID)
ROSS
SCRYMGEOUR
SINCLAIR
STEWART
SUTHERLAND
URQUHART
WALLACE

The list above gives only the main clans out of approximately 100, not all of which have Chiefs. For all the clans and septs see pages 185-189

Right, map from *The Historical Geography of the Clans of Scotland* by T. B. Johnston and Colonel James A. Robertson published in 1872.

MAP OF THE CLANS OF SCOTLAND

THE SCOTTISH TARTANS SOCIETY

One of the leading authorities on the subject of tartans and Highland dress is the Scottish Tartans Society, a charitable organization whose roots go back to the late 18th-century Highland Society, the 19th-century Celtic, Caledonian, Highland and St Andrews Societies, and the Tartan Society of Bannockburn. All these societies were instrumental in keeping alive an interest in 'the garb of old Gaul', an activity which was taken up by the Kilt Club and the Kilt Society before the First World War, neither of which survived for long.

However, towards the end of the Second World War, a Captain E. Matthew of the Black Watch proposed in a letter to the *Weekly Scotsman* that a society be formed 'to encourage generally the wearing of Highland dress . . . and to organise groups to discuss national and clan affairs', a project enthusiastically endorsed by Mr J. MacGregor Hastie in a further letter to that paper. Their hopes were not in fact to be fulfilled until nineteen years later, although their initiative was encouraged and kept alive by many enthusiasts and experts during this period, some of whom, like MacGregor Hastie, had extensive collections which were to help form the nucleus of the Society's own collection of tartans. Finally, in 1963, Captain Stuart Davidson from Stirling, who was also much interested in tartans and Highland dress, convened a meeting of a number of enthusiasts. Those present decided to set up the Scottish Tartans Information Centre, the initial aim of which was to identify tartans brought in by members. Their premises were two small rooms in the Tolbooth (jail) in Stirling, one of which had formerly been a cell for the aristocracy. The Scottish Tartans Society as it is known today was formally inaugurated in the Tolbooth by Lord Lyon King of Arms, Sir Thomas Innes of Learney, on 11 May 1963.

At the beginning, the information provided by the Society was based upon books on tartans, Scottish costume, genealogy and history which was soon supplemented by the purchase of Mr Hastie's collection of some 900 tartan samples. This collection was augmented by occasional purchases from commercial weavers while the documentary evidence available to the Society was greatly helped by the acquisition of the Wilson of Bannockburn papers. This early period in the Society's history was notable for the work done by D. C. Stewart, who started a system for recording tartans on index cards using two groups of three letters to describe the setts. It covered some 90 per cent of all tartans and, by adding an additional letter or number, could be used to cover them all.

The Society is now based in Comrie, a small weaving village west of Crieff situated at the foothills of the Scottish Highlands, where the weaving of tartans began in the 16th century and continued until the arrival of power-looms producing tartans in Glasgow in 1884, at which time there were 210 hand-loom weavers in the village. Housed in a merchant's house built in 1782, the Society's role as a museum – and as a working museum in the sense that the weaving of tartans is carried out within the premises – has been greatly expanded. The museum's display traces the development of tartan from its early history to the present day, and includes the double bar plaid woven in 1726 by Christine Young, 18th-century samples, records of almost every tartan woven since the Proscription and samples of most of them, and a piece of the tartan which Commander Alan L. Bean took to the moon in 1968. There are examples of Highland costume and important paintings, like that commissioned by Queen Victoria of her Highland servant, John Brown.

Despite the importance of the museum, however, the chief responsibility of the Society remains as it always was: to build up a definitive collection of tartans, monitor their use, advise on new tartan designs which are then added to the collection, and to disseminate information. To do this, the Society has to maintain a close relationship with the Standing Council of Chiefs (since the Highland Chiefs have the right to determine, *and change,* their tartans), the Court of Lord Lyon King of Arms, and anyone else wishing to be involved with tartans. It is frequently called upon to advise on difficult situations which can vary from the Duke of Argyll's refusal to recognize the current Campbell dress tartan, to the proposal by Ohio in the United States to adopt as its tartan a design that was similar to an existing Buchanan tartan, as a result of which the Society recommended changes to avoid confusion. Original research into all matters relating to Highland dress and tartans is constantly encouraged and undertaken by Fellows of the Society and recent research includes not only matters relating to the sett of tartans, but also such diverse topics as vegetable dyes, the sale and distribution of tartan cloth in Scotland during the period of proscription from 1746-1782, and rare portraiture of early Highlanders, both at home and abroad.

Commercial organizations are assisted and advised by the Society: Haig Whisky, for example, commissioned a new tartan without realizing that a Haig tartan already existed – even though it is unfortunately predominantly black and white, which are the colours of a rival brand! And the commercial clients are often overseas: the Society has been asked for advice from Japanese weavers, in which case it will authenticate design but not quality (though in fact Japanese tartans are usually of a very high quality) to fulfil its commitment to give the public some guarantee about the authenticity of the tartans they are buying.

However, while recording nearly 1,500 different setts and helping families and other bodies to acquire tartans of their own, the Society is also keen to avoid an unnecessary proliferation of tartans. Thus, when people called Stevenson complained that there was no tartan of that name, the Society pointed out that there is a Stephenson tartan which would meet their needs.

Today, both the Society and its museum are run by Dr Micheil MacDonald, who keeps in touch with the many Scottish societies throughout the world, and organizes exhibitions and lecture tours which have brought the work of the Scottish Tartans Society to the attention of some four million people in Asia, Australia, Europe and North America.

BRING FORRIT THE TARTAN

'Bring forrit the tartan', the motto of the Scottish Tartans Society, commemorates the occasion in November 1857 when General Sir Colin Campbell marched overnight with the 93rd Regiment (the Sutherland Highlanders) and the 4th Punjabi Regiment to lay seige to Secundrabagh, a stout fortress which 2,000 sepoys were defending. After the men of the 4th Punjabi had been engaged in a bloody but unsuccessful attack upon the 12-foot walls of the fort, Sir Colin finally called for the Sutherland Highlanders, who were massed on a small hill above. His command was historic:

'Bring forrit the tartan: let my ain lads at them!'

Without hesitation, the Scottish soldiers poured down the hillside and, after a breach had been made in the walls following a cannonade, retook the fort after hours of hand-to-hand fighting. The Scots won no less than six Victoria Crosses during the battle.

HIGHLAND GAMES

In Scotland, the wearing of the kilt is a fairly common sight, especially in the Highlands, and this tradition is also maintained by various regiments and military bands in other parts of the world where there is a strong Scottish influence. Scottish traditions are also kept alive by Clan Gatherings and Highland Games where tossing the caber, putting the shot, throwing the haggis and tug-'o-wars are usually among the more sporting events, and pipe band and Highland dancing competitions among the more artistic ones. These events often include other aspects of traditional Scottish music and song, followed by a ceilidh in the evening.

Such events may go back as far as the 12th and 13th centuries if their locality and date are based on medieval fairs. This is certainly true of the Lanark Lanimers, the Riding of the Marches in Annan, Dumfriesshire and the Langholm Common Riding in the Borders. There are several others, like the Inverkeithing Highland Games in Fife, whose records go back to the 17th century. But the majority of Highland Games in Scotland date from the 19th century and of these, there are quite a number, like the Highland Games in Tomintoul, Banffshire, that are almost 150 years old. The most important, of course, are the Games at Braemar, held in September. These are always attended by the Queen and other members of the Royal Family.

The tradition of Clan Gatherings and Highland Games is also maintained in Canada and the US. In Canada, for example, there are at least 12 major events held annually in Alberta, Manitoba, Nova Scotia, Ontario and Prince Edward Island, while in the US there are more than 100 events held right across the length and breadth of the country. Highland Clan Gatherings and Highland Games are also held annually in Western Australia, Queensland and New South Wales, Australia, and on both islands of New Zealand. There are also events in South Africa. Most feature the same activities as those in Scotland, and a number are marked by visits from Highland Chiefs from Scotland and elsewhere.

Since not all the locations and dates of Clan Gatherings and Highland Games are fixed from year-to-year, and the secretaries of Clan Societies, Caledonian Societies, St Andrew Societies and other interested bodies often change, it is not possible to give a list of events which would be accurate for more than a year at a time. So advice should be sought from the following:

SCOTLAND:

The Scottish Tartans Society, Comrie, Perthshire PH6 2DW

The Scottish Tourist Board, PO Box 705, Edinburgh (which publishes an annual list of events in Scotland)

CANADA:

Travel Alberta, PO Box 2500, Edmonton, Alberta T5J 2ZR

Tourism British Columbia, 1117 Wharf Street, Victoria, British Columbia V8W 2Z2

Travel Manitoba, Department 4020, Legislative Building, Winnipeg, Manitoba R3C OV8

Tourism New Brunswick, PO Box 12345, Fredericton, New Brunswick E3B 5C3

Tourism Branch, Department of Development, PO Box 2016, St John's, Newfoundland A1C 5R8

Travel Arctic, Yellowknife, Northwest Territories X1A 2L9

Department of Tourism, PO Box 130, Halifax, Nova Scotia B3J 2M7

Ontario Travel, 900 Bay Street, Queen's Park, Toronto M7A 2E5

Visitor Services Division, PO Box 940, Charlottetown, Prince Edward Island C1A 7M5

Tourisme Québec, CP 20 000, Québec G1K 7X2

SaskTravel, 3211 Alberta Street, Regina, Sasketchewan S4S 5W6

Tourism Yukon (CG), PO Box 2703, Whitehorse, Yukon Y1A 2C6

UNITED STATES

Delaware Free Press Inc, Building C, Suite 300, Greenville Center, 3801 Kennett Pike, Greenville, Delaware 19807

AUSTRALIA

Scottish Highland Games Association of Western Australia, 942 Albany Highway, East Victoria Park, Western Australia 6101

Australian Scots Association, 20 Newber Street, Sunnybank, Queensland 4109

Highland Society of New South Wales, 35 Bailey Street, West Mead, New South Wales 2145

NEW ZEALAND

Scottish Society of New Zealand, PO Box 936, Christchurch

Highland Pipe Bands Association, PO Box 2075, Christchurch

SOUTH AFRICA:

Transvaal Scottish Regiment, Old Bantu Commission Office, Malherbe Street, Newtown, Johannesburgh

ALPHABETICAL LIST OF FAMILY NAMES

Showing the Clan Tartans and Crests they are entitled to wear

Asterisk (*) indicates that the sept or family has a tartan of its own

FAMILY NAME	CONNECTED WITH CLAN
Abbot	Macnab
Abbotson	Macnab
*Abercombie	Family
Abernethy	Leslie
Adam	Gordon
Adamson	MacIntosh
Adie	Gordon
Airlie	Ogilvie
Alexander	MacAlister, MacDonald, MacDonell of Glengarry
Allan	MacDonald of Clanranald, MacFarlane
Allanson	MacDonald of Clanranald, MacFarlane
Allardice	Graham of Menteith
*Allison	Family
Alpin	MacAlpine
Anderson	Ross
Andrew	Ross
Angus	MacInnes
*Armstrong	Armstrong
Arthur	MacArthur
Austin	Keith
Ayson	MacIntosh or Shaw
*Baillie	Family
Bain	MacKay
*Baird	Baird
Bannatyne	Campbell of Argyll, Stewart of Bute
Bannerman	Forbes
Barclay	Barclay
Bard	Baird
Bartholomew	MacFarlane
Baxter	Macmillan
Bayne	Macbean, MacKay, Macnab
Bean	Macbean
Beath	MacDonald, Maclean of Duart
Beathy	MacBeth
Beaton	MacDonald, Maclean of Duart, MacLeod of Harris
Beton	MacDonald, MacLean, MacLeod of Harris
Bell	MacMillan
Begg	MacDonald or Drummond
Berkeley	Barclay
Bethune	MacDonald, MacLean, MacLeod of Harris
Beton	MacDonald, MacLean, MacLeod of Harris
Binnie	MacBean
Birrell	Birrell
Black	Lamont, MacGregor, MacLean of Duart
*Blair	Blair
Bontein, Bontine, Buntain, Bunten, Buntine	Graham of Menteith
Borthwick	Borthwick
Bouchannane	Buchanan
Bowie	MacDonald or Campbell
*Boyd	Stewart or Boyd
Brewer	Drummond, MacGregor
Brebner, Bremner	Farquharson
Brieve	Morrison
Brodie	Brodie
Broom	Sutherland
*Brown	Lamont, Macmillan

FAMILY NAME	CONNECTED WITH CLAN
Bruce, Brus	Bruce
Buchan	Cumin
Buchanan	Buchanan
Burdon	Lamont
Burk	MacDonald
*Burnett	Burnett
*Burnes, Burns	Campbell of Argyll
Caddell	Campbell of Cawdor
Caird	MacGregor, Sinclair
Calder	Campbell of Cawdor
Callum	MacLeod of Ramsay
Cameron	Cameron
Campbell	Campbell of Argyll
Campbell of Breadalbane	Campbell of Breadalbane
Campbell of Cawdor	Campbell of Cawdor
Campbell of Loudon	Campbell of Loudoun
Campbell of Strachur	MacArthur
Cariston	Skene
*Carmichael	MacDougall, Stewart of Appin
*Carnegie	Family
Carnie	Leslie, Skene
Carson	Macpherson, Galloway Gayre
Cattanach	Macpherson
Caw	MacFarlane
Chalmers	Cameron
Cheape	Cheape
Chesholme	Chisholm
Cheyne	Sutherland
Chisholm, Chisholme	Chisholm
*Christie	Ogilvie
*Clark, Clerk, Clarke	Cameron, MacIntosh, Macpherson
Clarkson	Cameron, MacIntosh, Macpherson
Clergy	Clergy
Clyne	Sinclair
*Cochrane	Family
*Cockburn	Family
Collier	Robertson
Colman	Buchanan
Colquhoun	Colquhoun
Colson	MacDonald or MacColl
Colyear	Robertson
Combich	Stewart of Appin
Combie	MacThomas
Comrie	MacGregor
Comyn, *see* Cumin	
Conacher	MacDougall
*Connall, Conne, Connell	MacDonald
Conochie	Campbell
Cook	Stewart of Bute
Coulson	MacDonald or MacColl
Couper, Cooper	Couper
Coutts	Farquharson
Cowan	Colquhoun, MacDougall
Craig	Craig
*Cranston	Family
*Crauford, Crawford	Lindsay
Crerar	MacIntosh
Combie	MacDonald
Crookshanks	Stewart of Atholl
Cruikshanks	Stewart of Atholl
Culchone	Colquhoun
Cumin or Cummin	Cumming
Cumming	Cumming
Cumyn	Cumming
Cunningham	Cunningham
Currie	MacDonald of Clanranald, Macpherson

FAMILY NAME	CONNECTED WITH CLAN
Dallas	MacIntosh
*Dalziel	Family
Dalzell, Daziel, Dalyell	Dalzell
Darroch	MacDonald
Davidson	Davidson
Davie	Davidson
Davis	Davidson
Davison	Davidson
Dawson	Davidson
*Deas	Deas
Denoon, Denune	Campbell of Argyll
Deuchar	Lindsay
Dewar	Macnab, Menzies
Dingwall	Munro, Ross
Dinnes	Innes
*Dis, Dise	Skene
Dochart	MacGregor
Doig	Graham of Monteith
Doles	MacIntosh
Donachie	Robertson
Donald	MacDonald
Donaldson	MacDonald
Donillson	MacDonald (of Antrim)
Donleavy, Donlevy	Buchanan
Dougall	MacDougall
Douglas	Douglas
Dove	Buchanan
Dow	Buchanan, Davidson
Dowall	MacDougall or Galloway
Dowe	Buchanan
Dowell	MacDougall
Drummond	Drummond
Drysdale	Douglas
Duff	MacDuff
Duffie, Duffy	Macfie
Dullach	Stewart of Atholl
*Dunbar	Family
Duncanson	Duncan
*Dundas	Dundas
Dunholme, Durham	Dunholme
Dunnachie	Robertson
*Dyce, Dys	Skene
Edie	Gordon
Elder	MacIntosh
Elphinstone	Elphinstone
Elliot	Elliot
Erskine	Erskine
Esson	MacIntosh or Shaw
Easson	MacIntosh or Shaw
Ewan, Ewen	MacEwen
Ewing	MacEwen
Fair	Ross
Farquhar	Farquharson
Farquharson	Farquharson
Federith	Sutherland
Fergus	Ferguson
Ferguson, Fergusson	Ferguson
Ferries	Ferguson
Ferson	Macpherson
Fiddes, Fettes	Fiddes
Fife	Macduff
Findlay, Finlay	Farquharson
Findlayson	Farquharson
Findlater	Ogilvie
Fleming	Murray
Fletcher	Fletcher, MacGregor
Forbes	Forbes
Fordyce	Forbes
*Forsyth	Family
Foulis	Munroe
France	Stewart (Ancient)
Fraser, Frazer	Fraser
Frescell, Friseal, Frizell	Fraser
Frew	Fraser

185

FAMILY NAME	CONNECTED WITH CLAN	FAMILY NAME	CONNECTED WITH CLAN	FAMILY NAME	CONNECTED WITH CLAN
Fullarton	Stewart of Bute	Hutchinson	MacDonald of Sleate	MacAlpin, MacAlpine	MacAlpine
Fyfe	MacDuff	Inches	Robertson	Macandeoir	Buchanan, Macnab, Menzies
Gair, Gayre	Gair, Gayre	*Inglis	Family		
*Galbraith	MacDonald, MarFarlane	Innes, Innie	Innes	*MacAndrew	Anderson
Gallie	Gunn	Isles	MacDonald of Sleate	MacAngus	MacInnes
Garrow	Stewart or Hay	*Irvine	Family	Macara	MacGregor
Gaunson	Gunn	Jameson, Jamieson	Gunn, Stewart	Macaree	MacGregor
Geddes	Gordon or Rose	*Jardine	Family	MacArthur	MacArthur or Campbell
Georgeson, George	Gunn	Johnson	Gunn, MacDonald of Glencoe	*MacAskill	MacLeod of Lewis
Gibb	Buchanan	*Johnston	Family	MacAslan	Buchanan
Gibson	Buchanan	Johnstoun	Johnston	MacAulay	MacAulay, MacLeod of Lewis
Gilbert	Buchanan	Kay	Davidson		
Gilbertson	Buchanan	Kean, Keene	Gunn, MacDonald of Glencoe	MacAuseln	Buchanan
Gilbride	MacDonald			MacAuslan, MacAusland	Buchanan
Gilchrist	MacLeachlan, Ogilvie	*Keith	Keith		
Gilfillan	Macnab	Kellie, Kelly	MacDonald	MacAuslane	Buchanan
Gillanders	Ross	Kendrick	Henderson, MacNaughton	MacAy	MacIntosh, Shaw
Gillespie	Macpherson	Kennedy	Kennedy	MacBain	Macbean
*Gillies	Macpherson	Kenneth	MacKenzie	MacBaxter	Macmillan
Gilmore	Morrison	Kennethson	MacKenzie	MacBean	MacBean
Gilroy	Grant	*Kerr	Kerr	*MacBeath	Macbean, MacDonald, MacLean
*Gladstone	Family	Kidd	Kidd		
Glen	MacIntosh	*Kilgour	Family	MacBeolain	MacKenzie
Glennie	MacIntosh	Kilpatrick	Colquhoun	*MacBeth	Macbean, MacDonald, MacLean
Gordon	Gordon	King	Macgregor		
Gorrie	MacDonald	Kinnell	Macdonald	MacBheath	MacBean, MacDonald, (Clan Donald, North and South), Maclean of Duart
Goudie	Macpherson	*Kinnieson	MacFarlane		
*Gow	Macpherson	Kirkpatrick	Colquhoun		
Gowan	MacDonald or Gow	Lachlan	MacLachlan	MacBrayne	MacNaughton
Gowrie	MacDonald	Lamb	Lamont	MacBride	MacDonald
Graham of Menteith	Graham of Menteith	Lambie	Lamont	MacBrieve	Morrison
		Lammie	Lamont	MacBurie	MacDonald of Clanranald
Graham of Montrose	Graham of Montrose	Lamond, Lamont	Lamont	MacCaa	MacFarlane
		Lamondson	Lamont	MacCaig	Farquharson, MacLeod of Harris
Graham	Graham of Menteith or Montrose	Landers	Lamont		
		Lang	MacDonald	MacCainsh	MacInnes
Grahame	Graham of Menteith or Montrose	Lasting	Lasting	MacCaishe	MacTavish
		*Lauder	Family	MacCall	MacAuley
Grant	Grant	Laurence	MacLaren	MacCallum	MacCallum
Grassich	Farquharson or Gordon	Law	MacLaren	MacCalman	Buchanan
Gray	Stewart of Atholl, Sutherland	Lean	MacLean	MacCalmont	Buchanan
		Leckie, Lecky	MacGregor	MacCamie	Stewart (Bute)
Gregor	MacGregor	Lees	Macpherson, Gillies	MacCammon, MacCammond	Buchanan
Gregorson	MacGregor	Lemond	Lamont		
Gregory	MacGregor	*Lennie, Lenny	Buchanan, Lennie	MacCansh	MacInnes
Greig	MacGregor	Lennox	MacFarlane, Stewart	MacCardney	Farquharson, MacIntosh
Greusach	Farquharson	*Leslie	Leslie	MacCartair, MacCarter	MacArthur
Grier or Grewar	MacGregor	Lewis	MacLeod of Lewis		
Grierson	MacGregor	Leys	Farquharson	MacCash	MacTavish
Griesck	MacFarlane	Limont, Limond	Lamont	*MacCaskill	MacLeod of Lewis
Grigor	MacGregor	Lindsay	Lindsay	MacCaul	MacDonald
Gruamach	MacFarlane	Linklater	Sinclair	MacCause	MacFarlane
Gunn	Gunn	*Livingston, Livingstone	Stewart of Appin	MacCaw	Stewart of Bute or Farquharson
Guthrie	Family				
*Haig	Family	*Lobban	Logan	MacCay	MacKay
Hallyard	Skene	Logan	Maclennan	MacCeallaich	MacDonald
Hamilton	Hamilton	Loudon	Campbell	MacClerich	Cameron, MacIntosh
Hardie, Hardy	Farquharson, MacIntosh McHardy	Love	MacKinnon	MAcChlery	Macpherson
		Low	MacLaren	MacChoiter	MacGregor
Harper	Buchanan	Lowrie	Maclaren	MacChruiter	Buchanan
Harperson	Buchanan	Lucas, Luke	Lamont	MacCloy	Stewart (Bute)
Hawes, Haws or Hawson	Campbell	*Lumsden	Forbes	MacClure	MacLeod of Harris
		Lyall	Sinclair	MacClymont	Lamont
Hawthorn	MacDonald	Lyon	Farquharson, Lamont	MacCodrum	MacConald
Hay	Hay	Mac a'Challies	MacDonald	*MacColl	MacDonald, MacColl
*Henderson	Gunn, Henderson	Macachounich	Colquhoun	MacColman	Buchanan
Hendrie, Hendry	Henderson, MacNaughton	MacAdam	MacGregor	MacComas	Gunn
Hewison	MacDonald	MacAdie	Ferguson	MacCombe	MacThomas
*Home, Hume	Family	MacAindra	MacFarlane	MacCombich	Stewart of Appin
Hope	Hope	MacAlaster	MacAlister	MacCombie	MacThomas
Houston	MacDonald of Sleate	Macaldonach	Buchanan	MacComie	MacThoms
Howison	MacDonald of Sleate	Macalduie	Lamont	MacConacher	MacDougall
Hughson	MacDonald of Sleate	MacAlester	MacAlister	MacConachie	Robertson
*Hunter	Kerr	MacAlister	MacAlister	MacConchy	Mackintosh
Huntly	Gordon	MacAllan	MacDonald of Clanranald, MacFarlane	MacCondy	MacFarlane
Hutcheonson	MacDonald of Sleate			MacConnach	MacKenzie
Hutcheson, Hutchison	MacDonald of Sleate	MacAllaster	MacAlister	MacConnechy	Campbell, Robertson
		MacAllister	MacAlister	MacConnell	MacDonald

186

FAMILY NAME	CONNECTED WITH CLAN	FAMILY NAME	CONNECTED WITH CLAN	FAMILY NAME	CONNECTED WITH CLAN
MacConnichie	Campbell, Robertson	MacFergus	Ferguson	Macilwraith	MacDonald
MacCooish	MacDonald	Macfie or Macfee	Macfie	Macilzegowie	Lamont
MacCook	MacDonald	*MacGaskill	MacLeod of Lewis	Macimmey	Fraser
MacCorkill	Gunn	MacGaw	MacFarlane	Macinally	Buchanan
MacCorkindale	MacCorquodale	MacGeachie	MacDonald of Clanranald	Macindeor	Buchanan, Macnab, Menzies
MacCorkle	Gunn	MacGeacin	MacDonald of Clanranald		
MacCormack	Buchanan	MacGeoch	MacFarlane	Macindoe	Buchanan
MacCormick	Maclaine of Lochbuie	Macghee, Macghie	Mackay	Macinnes	Macinnes
*MacCorquodale	Family	MacGibbon	Buchanan, Campbell of Argyll, Graham of Menteith	*Macinroy	Robertson
MacCorrie, MacCorry	Macquarrie			Macinstalker	MacFarlane
				Macintosh	Macintosh
MacCoull	MacDougall, Galloway	MacGilbert	Buchanan	Macintyre	Macintyre
MacCowan	Colquhoun, MacDougall	MacGilchrist	MacLachlan, Ogilvie	MacIock	MacFarlane
Macracken	Maclean	*MacGill	Galloway and MacGill	MacIsaac	Campbell, MacDonald of Clanranald
MacCrae, MacCrea	Macrae	MacGilledow	Lamont		
		MacGillegowie	Lamont	*MacIver or MacIvor	Campbell of ARgyll, Robertson of Stuan MacKenzie
MacCrain	MacDonald	MacGillivantic	MacDonald of Keppoch		
MacCraw	Macrae	MacGillivoor	MacGillivray		
MacCreath	Macrae	MacGillivray	MacGillivray	MacJames	MacFarlane
MacCrie	MacKay, Macrae	MacGillonie	Cameron	MacKail	Cameron, MacColl
MacCrimmon	Macleod of Harris	MacGilp	MacDonell of Keppoch	MacKames	Gunn
MacCrowther	MacGregor	MacGilroy	Grant	Mackay	Mackay
MacCuag	MacDonald	MacGilvernock	Graham of Menteith	MacKeachan	MacDonald of Clanranald
MacCuaig	Farquharson, MacLeod of Harris	MacGilvra	MacGillivray, Maclaine of Lochbuie	MacKeamish	Gunn
				MacKean	Gunn, MacDonald of Ardnamurchan
MacCuish	MacDonald	MacGilvray	MacGillivray		
MacCuithein	MacDonald	Macglashan	MacIntosh Stewart (Atholl)	Mackechnie	MacDonald of Clanranald
MacCulloch	MacDonald, MacDougall, Munro, Ross	Macglasrich	MacIver, MacDonell of Keppoch	Mackee	MacKay of Galloway
				Mackeygie	MacIntosh
MacCunn	MacQueen	MacGorrie, MacGorry	MacDonald, MacQuarrie	MacKeith	Keith, Macpherson
MacCurrach	Macpherson			MacKellachie	MacDonald
MacCutchen, MacCutsheon	MacDonald of Sleate	MacGory	MacLaren	MacKellaig	MacDonald
		MacGowan	MacDonald	MacKellaigh	MacDonald
Macdaid, Macdade	Davidson	MacGoun, MacGown	MacDonald, Macpherson	*MacKellar	Campbell of Argyll
MacDaniell	MacDonald			MacKelloch	MacDonald
MacDavid	Davidson	MacGrath	Macrae	MacKenmie	Fraser
*MacDermaid, MacDermid, MacDiarmid	Campbell of Argyll	MacGregor	MacGregor	MacKennie	
		MacGrigor	MacGregor	*MacKendrick, see Henderson	
		MacGreusich	Buchanan, MacFarlane		
MacDonachie	Robertson	Macgrime	Graham of Menteith	MacKenrick	MacNaughton, Henderson
MacDonald	MacDonald	*MacGrory	MacGregor, MacRory	MacKenzie	MacKenzie
MacDonald of Ardnamurchan	MacDonald of Ardnamurchan	Macgrowther	MacGregor	MacKeochan	MacDonald of Clanranald
		Macgruder	MacGregor	MacKerchar	Farquharson
MacDondald of Clanranald	MacDonald of Clanranald	Macguer	Fraser	MacKerlich	MacKenzie
		Macgruther	MacGregor	MacKerachar	Farquharson
MacDonald of the Isles and of Sleat	MacDonald of the Isles and of Sleat	MacGuaig	Farquharson	MacKerras	Ferguson
		MacGuaran	MacQuarrie	MacKersey	Ferguson
MacDonleavy	Buchanan	MacGuffie	Macfie	MacKessock	Campbell MacDonald of Clanranald
MacDonell of Glengarry	MacDonnell of Glengarry	MacGugan, MacGuigan	MacDougall, MacNeill		
				MacKichan	MacDougall
MacDonnell of Keppoch	MacDonnell of Keppoch	MacGuire	MacQuarrie	Mackie	Mackay
		Machaffie	Macfie	MacKiggan	MacDonald
MacDougall	MacDougall	*Machardie, Machardy	Farquharson, MacIntosh	MacKillican	MacIntosh
MacDowall, MacDowell	MacDougall and Galloway			MacKillip	MacDonell of Keppoch
		MacHarold	MacLeod of Harris	MacKillop	
Macdrain	MacDonald	MacHay	MacIntosh, Shaw	MacKim	Fraser
MacDuff	MacDuff	MacHendrie		MacKimmie	Fraser
MacDuffie	Macfie	MacHendry	Henderson, MacNaughton	Macindlay	Farquharson
MacDulothe	MacDougall	MacHenry		*Mackinlay	Buchanan, Farquharson, MacFarlane, Stewart
MacEachan	MacDonald of Clanranald	MacHowell	MacDougall		
MacEachern, MacEachran	MacDonald	MacHugh	MacDonald of Sleate	Mackinley	Buchanan
		MacHutchen, MacHutcheon	MacDonald of Sleate	Mackinnell	MacDonald
MacEachin	MacDonald of Clanranald			Mackinney	MacKenzie
MacEaracher	Farquharson	*MacIan	Gunn, MacDonald of Ardnamurchan	Mackinning	Mackinnon
MacElfrish	MacDonald			Macintosh	Mackintosh
MacElheran	MacDonald	Macildowie	Cameron	MacKintosh see MacIntosh	
MacEoin	MacFarlane	Macilduy	MacGregor, MacLean of Duart		
Maceol	MacNaughton			Mackinven	Mackinnon
MacErracher	Farquharson, MacFarlane	Macilleriach	MacDonald	*MacKirdy	Stewart (Bute)
MacEwan or MacEwen	MacEwan	Macilreach	MacDonald	MacKissock	Campbell, MacDonald of Clanranald
		Macilrevie	MacDonald		
*MacFadyen, MacFadzean	Maclaine of Lochbuie	Macilriach	MacDonald	Macknight	MacNaughton
		Macilroy	Grant	MacLachlan	MacLachlan
MacFall	MacIntosh	Macilvain	Macbean	*Maclae	Stewart of Appin, MacLay
MacFarlan	MacFarlane	Macilvora	Maclaine of Lochbuie	Maclagan	Robertson
MacFarlane	MacFarlane	Macilvrae	MacGillivray	MacLaghlan	MacLachlan
MacFarquhar	Farquharson	Macilvride	MacDonald	Maclaine	Maclaine of Lochbuie
MacFater	MacLaren	Macilwham	Lamont	MacLairish	MacDonald
MacFeat	MacLaren	Macilwhom	Lamont	MacLamond	Lamont

187

FAMILY NAME	CONNECTED WITH CLAN	FAMILY NAME	CONNECTED WITH CLAN	FAMILY NAME	CONNECTED WITH CLAN
MacLardie, MacLardy	MacDonald	MacNeil of Barra and Gigha	MacNeil of Barra, McNeill of Gigha	MacTear	Macintyre, Ross
MacLaren	MacLaren	MacNish	MacGregor	*MacThomas	MacThomas
MacLarty	MacDonald	MacNiter	MacFarlane	MacTier, MacTire	Ross
MacLauchlan	MacLachlan	MacNiven	Cumin, MacIntosh, MacNaughton	MacUlric	Kennedy
MacLaughlan	MachLachlan			MacUre	Campbell of Argyll, MacIver
MacLaurin	Maclaren	MacNuir	MacNaughton	Macvail	Cameron, MacKay, MacIntosh, Macpherson
MacLaverty	MacDonald	MacNuyer	Buchanan, MacFarlane, MacNaughton		
MacLaws	Campbell			MacVanish	MacKenzie
*Maclay, Macleay	Stewart of Appin	MacOmie	MacThoms	MacVarish	MacDonald of Clanranald
MacLean	Maclean	MacOmish	Gunn	MacVeagh, McVey	MacDonald, MacLean
MacLehose	Campbell, Galloway	MacOnie	Cameron		
*MacLeish	Macpherson, Gillies	MacOran	Campbell of Argyll	MacVean	Macbean
MacLeister	Fletcher	MacO'Shannaig	MacDonald of Kintyre	MacVey	MacDonald, MacLean
*MacLellan	Galloway	Macoul, Macowl	MacDougall, Galloway	MacVicar	Campbell, MacNaughton
*MacLennan, see Logan	MacLennan	MacOurlic	Kennedy	MacVinish	MacKenzie
		MacOwen	Campbell	MacVurie	MacDonald of Clanranald
MacLeod of Harris	MacLeod of Harris	MacPatrick	Lamont, MacLaren	MacVurrich	MacDonald of Clanranald, Macpherson
MacLeod of Lewes	MacLeod of Lewes	MacPeter	MacGregor		
MacLergain	MacLean	*MacPhail	Cameron, MacIntosh, MacKay	MacWalrick	Kennedy
Maclerie	Cameron, MacIntosh, Macpherson			MacWalter	MacFarlane
		MacPhater	MacLaren	MacWattie	Buchanan
MacLeverty	MacDonald	MacPhedran	Campbell, Macaulay	MacWhannell	MacDonald
MacLewis	MacLeod of Lewis, Stewart	MacPhedron	MacAulay	MacWhirr	MacQuarrie
*MacLintoch	Family, MacDougall	Macphee, Macphie, see Macfie		MacWhirter	Buchanan
MacLise	Macpherson, Gillies			*MacWilliam	Gunn, MacFarlane
MacLiver	MacGregor			Malcolm	Maccallum
MacLoy	Stewart of Bute	MacPheidiran	MacAulay	Malcolmson	Maccallum, MacLeod
MacLucas	Lamont, MacDougall	MacPherson	Macpheron		Malcom
MacLugash	MacDougall	MacPhilip	MacDonell of Keppoch	Malloch	MacGregor
MacLulich	MacDougall, Munro, Ross	MacPhorich	Lamont	Mann	Gunn
Maclure	MacLeod of Harris	MacPhun	Campbell, Matheson	Manson	Gunn
MacLymont	Lamont	Macquaire	Macquarrie	Mar(r)	Mar
MacMartin	Cameron	Macquarrie	Macquarrie	Marnoch	Innes
MacMaster	Buchanan, MacInnes	Macqueen	Macqueen	Marshall	Keith
MacMath	Matheson	Macquey	MacKay	Martin	Cameron, MacDonald
MacMaurice	Buchanan	Macquhirr	MacQuarrie	Masterson	Buchanan
MacMenzies	Menzies	Macquire	Macquarrie	Matheson, Matheison	Matheson
MacMichael	Stewart (Appin)	MacQuistan	MacDonald		
Macmillan	Macmillan	MacQuisten	MacDonald	Mathie	Matheson
MacMinn	Menzies	Macquoid	MacKay	Mavor	Innes, Urquhart
MacMonies	Menzies	Macra	Macrae	*Maxwell	Family
MacMorran	Mackinnon	Macrach	Macrae	May	MacDonald
MacMunn	Stewart (Ancient)	Macrae	Macrae	Means	Menzies
MacMurchie, MacMurchy	Buchanan, MacDonald, MacKenzie	Macraild	MacLeod of Harris	Meikleham	Lamont
		MacRaith	MacDonald, Macrae	Mein, Meine	Menzies
MacMurdo	MacDonald, Macpherson	MacRanald	MacDonald, Keppoch	*Melville	Family
MacMurdoch	MacDonald, Macpherson	MacRankin	MacLean	Melvin	Meville
MacMurray	Galloway	MacRath	Macrae	Mengues	Menzies
MacMurrich	MacDonald of Clanranald, Macpherson	MacRitchie	MacIntosh	Mennie	Menzies
		MacRob, MacRobb	Gunn, Innes, MacFarlane, Robertson	Menteith	Graham, Stewart (Ancient)
MacMutrie	Stewart (Bute)			Menzies	Menzies
Macnab	MacNab	MacRobbie	Robertson	Meynars, Meyners	Menzies
MacNachdan	MacNaughton	MacRobert,	Robertson	Michie	MacDonald, Keppoch
MacNachton	MacNaughton	MacRobie	Drummond, Robertson	*Middleton	Innes
MacNaghten	MacNaughton	*MacRorie, MacRory	MacDonald	Mill, Milne	Innes, Ogilvie
MacNair, MacNayer	MacFarlane, MacNaughton, Weir			Miller, Millar	MacFarlane
		*MacRuer	MacDonald	Milne-Gordon	Innes, Ogilvie
MacNamell	MacDougall	*MacRurie, MacRury	MacDonald	Minn	Menzies
MacNauchton	MacNaughton			Minnus	Menzies
MacNaughtan	MacNaughton	MacShannachan	MacDonald	*Mitchell	Innes
MacNaughton	MacNaughton	MacShimes	Fraser	*Moir	Gordon, Muir
MacNayer	MacNaughton	MacShimmie	Fraser	Monach	MacFarlane
MacNeal	MacNeil of Barra, McNeil of Gigha	MacSimon	Fraser	Monro or Monroe	Munro
		MacSorley	Cameron, Lamont, MacDonald	Monteith	Graham, Stewart (Ancient)
MacNee	MacGregor			Montgomerie	Montgomerie
MacNeil	MacNeil of Barra, McNeill of Gigha	MacSporran	MacDonald	Monzie	Menzies
		MacSuain	MacQueen	Morran	Mar
McNeil	McNeill of Gigha	MaSwan	MacDonald, MacQueen	Moray	Murray
MacNeilage	MacNeill	MacSween, MacSwen	MacQueen	More	Leslie
MacNeiledge	MacNeill			Morgan (Scottish)	MacKay
McNeill	McNeill of Gigha	MacSwyde	MacQueen	Morison, Morrison	Morrison
MacNeish	MacGregor	MacSymon	Fraser		
MacNelly	MacNeil	*MacTaggart	Ross	*Mowat	Sutherland
MacNeur	MacFarlane	MacTary	Innes	*Muir	Family
MacNicol	MacNicol, Nicolson	MacTause	Campbell of Argyll, MacTavish	Munn	Stewart of Bute
MacNichol	Campbell of Argyll			Munro or Munroe	Munro
MacNider	MacFarlane	*MacTavish	Campbell of Argyll, MacTavish	Murchie	Buchanan, MacDonald, MacKenzie
MacNie	MacGregor				

FAMILY NAME	CONNECTED WITH CLAN	FAMILY NAME	CONNECTED WITH CLAN	FAMILY NAME	CONNECTED WITH CLAN
Murchison	Buchanan, MacDonald, MacKenzie	Robb	MacFarlane, Robertson	Tarrill	MacIntosh
Murdoch	MacDonald, Macpherson	Robertson	Robertson	Tawesson	Campbell of Argyll, MacTavish
Murdoson	MacDonald, Macpherson	Robinson	Gunn	Tawse	Farquharson, MacTavish
Murray	Murray (Atholl and Tullibardine)	Robson	Gunn	*Taylor (Scots)	Cameron
		Rob Roy	MacGregor	*Tennant	Family
Nairn	Nairn	*Rollo	Family	Thomas (Scots)	Campbell of Argyll, MacThomas
*Napier	MacFarlane	Ronald	MacDonell of Keppoch	Thomason	Campbell of Argyll, MacThomas
Neal	MacNeil	Ronaldson	MacDonell of Keppoch		
Neil, Neill	MacNeil	Rorison	MacDonald, MacRory	Thompson	Campbell of Argyll
Neilson	MacKay, MacNeill	Rose	Rose	*Thomson	MacThomas
Neish	MacGregor	Ross	Ross	Thoms	MacThomas
Nelson	Gunn	Roy	Robertson	Todd	Gordon
Nicol, Nicoll, Nicholl	MacNicol	Ruskin	Buchanan	Tolmie	MacLeod
*Nicolson see MacNicol		*Russell	Family	Tonnochy	Robertson
		*Ruthven	Family	Tosh	MacIntosh
*Nisbet	Family	Sanderson	MacDonnell of Glengarry	Toshach	MacIntosh
Neish	MacGregor	Sandison	Gunn	Tough	Mar
Niven	Cumin, MacIntosh, MacNaughton	Scobie	Mackay	Toward, Towart	Lamont
		Scott	Scott	Train	MacDonald
Noble	MacIntosh	*Seton, Seaton	Seton	Turner	Lamont
Norman	MacLeod of Harris	Shannon	MacDonald	Tweedie	Fraser
O'Drain	MacDonald	Shaw	Shaw	Tyre	MacIntyre
Ogilvie, Ogilvy	Ogilvie	Sim, Sime	Fraser	Ure	Campbell of Argyll, MacIver
*Oliphant	Sutherland	Simon	Fraser		
O'May	MacDonald	Simpson	Fraser	Urquhart	Urquhart
O'Shaig	MacDonald	Sinclair	Sinclair	Vass	Munro, Ross
O'Shannachan	MacDonald	Skene	Skene	Vipont	Vipont
O'Shannaig	MacDonald	Small	Murray	Walker	Stewart of Appin MacGregor
Parlane	MacFarlane	Smith (Scots)	Clan Chattan, Gow		
Paterson	MacLaren	Somerville	Somerville	Wallis, Wallace	Wallace
Patrick	Lamont	Sorley	Cameron, Lamont, MacDonald	Waggrill	Waggrill
Paul	Cameron, MacIntosh, MacPhail, MacKay	Spalding	Murray	Walters	Forbes, Buchanan
		*Spence, Spens	MacDuff	Wass	Munro, Ross
Peter	MacGregor	Spittal or Spittel	Buchanan	*Watson	Buchanan
Philipson	MacDonell of Keppoch	Sporran	MacDonald	Watt	Buchanan
Pitullich	MacDonald	Stalker	MacFarlane	Weaver	MacFarlane
Polson	MacKay	Stark	Robertson	*Weir	Buchanan, MacFarlane, MacNaughton
Purcell	MacDonald	Steuart, Stuart	Stewart, Ancient		
*Rae	Macrae	Stewart of Appin	Stewart of Appin	*Wemyss	Macduff, Wemyss
*Raeburn	Family	Stewart of Atholl	Stewart of Atholl	Whannell	MacDonald, Galloway
Ramsay	Ramsay	Stewart of Galloway	Stewart of Galloway	Wharrie	Macquarrie
Rankin	MacLean	Stewart, Royal	Stewart, Royal	White, Whyte	Lamont, MacGregor
*Rattray	Family	Strachan	Mar	Will	Gunn
Reid	Robertson	Stuart of Bute	Stuart of Bute	Williamson	Gunn, MacKay
Reoch	Farquharson, MacDonald	*Sturrock	Family, Ogilvie	*Wilson	Gunn
Revie	MacDonald	Sutherland	Sutherland	*Wotherspoon	Family
Riach	Farquharson, MacDonald	Swan	MacQueen	Wright	Macintyre
Rich	Rich	Swanson	Gunn	Wylie	Gunn, MacFarlane, MacWilliam
Rish	Buchanan	Syme	Fraser		
Risk	Buchanan	Symon	Fraser	Yuill, Yuille, Yule	Buchanan
Ritchie	MacIntosh	*Taggart	Ross, MacTaggart		

BIBLIOGRAPHY

Many of the books mentioned in this list are long since out of print but it is hoped that the interested reader may be able to track down some of them.

Clans and Tartans (booklet in series: 'Introducing Scotland') by Roderick Martine, Spur Books, UK
Clans Septs & Regiments of the Scottish Highlands by Frank Adam, 1934, revised 1970, Johnston & Bacon, Edinburgh & London
The Clans and Tartans of Scotland by Robert Bain, 1938, Collins/Fontana, London
The Clans of the Highlands of Scotland by Thomas Smibert, 1850
The Costumes of Scotland by J. Telfer Dunbar, 1981, Batsford, London
The Guide to Scottish Tartans, 1977, Shepheard-Walwyn, London
Heraldic Standards and Other Ensigns by Robert Gayne, 1959, Oliver & Boyd, Edinburgh
The Highland Clans by Sir Iain Moncrieffe of that Ilk, 1967, Barrie & Rockcliffe, London
Highland Folk Ways (an excellent book with a good chapter on Highland fabrics) by I. F. Grant, Routledge & Kegan Paul, London
History of Highland Dress (some editions of this book have an excellent appendix on 'Early Scottish Highland Dyes' by Annnette Kok) by J. Telfer Dunbar, 1962 & 1979, Oliver & Boyd and Batsford, London
The Land of the Gael by John Ross, 1930
Lichens for Vegetable Dyeing by Eileen Bolton, Studio Vista, London, Robin & Russ Handweavers, US
Memoirs of a Highland Lady by E. Grant, 1898
The Official Tartan Map (a wall chart of approved tartans and their thread counts) by J. Telfer Dunbar and Don Pottinger, Elm Tree Books (Hamish Hamilton), London
Old and Rare Scottish Tartans (illustrated by woven silk examples of tartan setts) by Donald William Stewart, 1893
Scotland's Clans and Tartans by James D. Scarlett, 1974 & 1981, Lutterworth, Guildford and Shepeard-Walwyn, London
Scotland's Forged Tartans (an analysis of the *Vestiarium Scoticum* Mystery) by J. Charles Thompson and D. C. Stewart, Paul Harris Publishing, Edinburgh
Scots Heraldry by Sir Thomas Innes of Learney, 1956 & 1978, Oliver & Boyd, Edinburgh, Johnston & Bacon, London
Scottish Clans and Tartans by Ian Grimble, 1977, Hamlyn Paperbacks, London
Scottish Family Histories by Joan P. S. Ferguson, 1960, Scottish Central Library, Edinburgh
Scottish Family History by Margaret Stuart and Sir James Balfour Paul, 1930, Oliver & Boyd, Edinburgh
The Scottish Gael by James Logan, 1931
The Setts of the Scottish Tartans (the most comprehensive collection of thread counts and details of tartans) by Donald C. Stewart, 1950 & 1974, Oliver & Boyd, Edinburgh, Shepheard-Walwyn, London
Simple Heraldry by Iain Moncrieffe and Don Pottinger, 1953, Nelson, Walton-on-Thames
'So You're Going to Wear the Kilt' by J. Charles Thompson, 1979 & 1981, Paul Harris Publishing, Edinburgh
Spinning Wheels, Spinners & Spinning (a comprehensive historical and practical book) by Patricia Baines, Batsford, London
The Surnames of Scotland by George F. Black, 1946, New York Public Library
Tartans: Pleasures and Treasures by Lady Christian Hesketh, Weidenfeld & Nicolson, London
The Tartans of the Clans and Families of Scotland by Sir Thomas Innes of Learney, 1938, Johnston & Bacon, London
The Tartans of the Scottish Clans by James D. Scarlett, 1975, Collins, London
The Tartan Spotter's Guide by James D. Scarlett and Angus McBride, 1973, Shepheard-Walwyn, London
The World Directory of Scottish Associations, Cassell Ltd, London

INDEX

Bold type denotes tartans illustrated with a colour photograph

Abercrombie tartan, chart of sett, 54
Aberdeen tartan, Wilson's List 1819, 23; district tartan, 172
Acton, early coat, 13
Agnew tartan, 178
Allan, John & Charles (see: Sobieski Brothers)
Allison tartan, chart of sett, 54
alternative fibres for weaving tartans, 34
American tartans: Georgia, 174-175; Ohio, 183
ancient colours, 45, 52
Anderson tartan, chart of sett, 54
Angus tartan, chart of sett, 54; 172
Applecross tartan, 172
Arbuthnot tartan, chart of sett, 54; 178
Armstrong tartan, chart of sett, 54
Ard-righ (clan chief), 10, 13, 158
Arferille, Nicolay d', description of Highlands (1582), 13-14
Argyll tartan, 173
Argyll & Sutherland Highlanders, tartan, 163, 168
Arran tartan, 172
asymmetric sett, explanation, 53
Atholl Highlanders tartan, 168
Baillie tartan, Wilson's tartan list 1819, 23; chart of sett, 55
balanced cloth, 31, 46
Balmoral tartan, 29, 163
Barclay tartan, dress & hunting, chart of sett, 55
Bean, Commander Alan L., astronaut, 182
Benbecula, song describing tartan sett, 31
Birral tartan, Wilson's tartan list 1819, 23; chart of sett, 55
Black Watch tartan, 29, 163, 165, 166, 168
Blair tartan, chart of sett, 55
Blair Logie tartan, 172
blue/green tartans, 172
bonnet, 13, 14, 15, 16, 19, 170, 171
Border tartan, 173
Borland, John & Bella (see: 'The Weavers of Kilbarchan')
Borthwick & Borthwich dress tartan, chart of sett, 58
Bowie tartan, chart of sett, 58
Boyd tartan, chart of sett 58; 178
brat (mantle), 10
breacan (check), 10, 13
britch, part of a fleece, 35
Brodie, dress & hunting tartan, chart of sett, 58
Bruce, New tartan, Wilson's tartan list 1819, 23
Bruce, Old tartan, Wilson's tartan list 1819, 23; chart of sett, 58
Bruce of Kinnaird tartan, chart of sett, 59
Buchan tartan, chart of sett, 59, 173
Buchanan tartan, woven in Kilbarchan, 51; chart of sett, 59, 140
Buchanan hunting tartan, chart of sett, 59
Buchanan, George, 'Rerum Scoticarium Historia (1582), description of Highlanders dress, 14
Burnett tartan, chart of sett, 59
Caledonia tartan, Wilson's tartan list 1819, 23
Cameron Highlanders, 170
Cameron tartan, chart of sett, 62; 178
Cameron hunting tartan, chart of sett, 62
Cameron of Lochiel tartan, chart of sett, 62

Campbell tartan, 172; refusal of chief to recognise dress tartan, 183
Campbell of Argyll, or Campbell of Lochawe tartan, chart of sett, 62
Campbell of Breadalbane, chart of sett, 62
Campbell of Cawdor, chart of sett, 62
Campbell of Loudon, chart of sett, 62
Canadian tartans, 174, 178
carding, 34
carders, 36
Carmichael tartan, chart of sett, 63
Carnegie tartan, chart of sett, 63
Carrick tartan, 172
cath-dath, coarse cloth, 13
Charles Edward Stuart, Prince: his style of dress, 18-20; his reputed grandsons, 24; his tartans, 163
Chattan tartan, description of portrait of 19th chief, 18; chart of sett, 63; 178
Chisholm tartan, chart of sett, 63
Christie tartan, chart of sett, 63
Church (Clergy), references to early Highland clergy dress, 12; special sett, 13; chart of sett, 63
Clanedin tartan, 172
Clans: association with tartans, 10; destruction of clan system, 18; clan gathering 1822, 23; clan chiefs control on tartans, 29; looking up clan tartans, 52; clan tartan list, 185
Cochran tartan, chart of sett, 63; 178
Cockburn tartan, chart of sett, 63
colours: natural fleece colours, 40; reds & purples from plants, 42; yellows & browns from plants, 42; blues from plants, 43; greens from plants, 45; black from plants, 45; 'old' colours, 45
Colquhoun tartan, chart of sett, 63
combing, preparing fibres, 36
Comrie, home of Scottish Tartans Society & museum, 182
Comyn (or Cumming) tartan, chart of sett, 66
Cooper tartan, chart of sett, 66
Craig tartan, chart of sett, 66
Cranstoun (or Cranston) tartan, chart of sett, 66
Crawford tartan, chart of sett, 67
Crieff tartan, Wilson's tartan list 1819, 23; chart of sett, 67; district tartan, 172
Cromarty MS: description & origin, 24; authenticity, 25; analysis, 26
crotal (or crottle): see Lichens
Culloden, Battle of; 18, 19, 23, 25, 165; tartan, 173
Cunningham tartan, chart of sett, 67; 173
Dalriada, Kingdom 7th century A.D., 10
Dalzell tartan, chart of sett, 67
Davidson tartan, chart of sett, 67; 178
Deeside tartan, 172
Defoe, Daniel; extract from 'Memories of a Cavalier' (1639), 164
design, of tartan, 48-49
De Vita Sua (1104-1112) by Guibert of Nogent, description of Scots, 12
diamond, part of a fleece, 35
Disarming Acts, 1725 & 1746, 20-21
District tartans, 172-173
Douglas tartans, green & grey; chart of sett, 67
drop-spindle (Gaelic: fearsaid); description & use in spinning, 38
Drumlithie tartan, 173
Drummond tartan; New Bruce, 23
Drummond of Perth tartan; chart of sett, 70; connection to Prince Charles Edward, 163
Dunbar, J. Telfer: extract from writings on district tartans, 172
Dunbar tartan: chart of sett, 70; 173
Dunblane tartan: chart of sett, 70; 173

Duncan tartan: chart of sett, 70
Dundas tartan: chart of sett, 71
Dundee tartan, Wilson's tartan list 1819, 23; district tartan, 172
Dyce tartan: chart of sett, 71
dyes and dyeing, 40-41
Edinburgh tartan, 172
Eglinton tartan, 173
Elliot tartan: spelling of name in verse, 52; chart of sett, 71
Erracht Cameron Q.O.H. tartan, 169
Erskine tartan; chart of sett, 71, 49
Farquharson tartan: chart of sett, 71; 178
fashions in tartans, 45
Ferguson of Athol tartan: chart of sett, 74
Ferguson of Balquihidder: chart of sett, 74
filibeg (kilt); 14, 23
fleece: sorting, 35; plucked for worsted spinning, 36; properties of Highland and Lowland fleece, 40
Fletcher, Fletcher of Dunans, Flesher tartan: chart of sett, 74
flyer wheel, 38-39
Forbes, Bishop Robert; collector of Prince Charles Edward mementoes, 20
Forbes (ancient) tartan, 178
Forbes tartan: chart of sett, 74
Forbes dress tartan: chart of sett, 75
Foreign tartans: 23; Norway, Netherlands, Portugal, Morocco, India, Pakistan, Bangladesh, Malaysia, Oman, Dubai, Canada, U.S.A., 174
Forsyth tartan: chart of sett, 75
Fort William tartan: Wilson's tartan list 1819, 23; district tartan, 172
Fraser, James: Highland dress, 26
Fraser tartan: chart of sett, 75
Fraser of Lovat tartan, chart of sett, 48, 75
Gael (Scotland), 10
Gala Water tartan, 172
Galbraith tartan, chart of sett, 78
Gallowater tartan: Wilson's tartan list 1819, 23; chart of sett, 78
Galloway tartan: chart of sett, 78
gallowglasses, Scottish mercenaries: 13
Gayre, dress tartan, 178
George II, King, 18
George IV, King; visit to Scotland 1822, 23, 158
Georgia tartan, 174, 176
Ghurka tartan, 174
Gillies (Macleish): chart of sett, 78
Glasgow tartan, 172
Glen Lyon tartan, 172
Glen Orchy tartan, 172
Gordon tartan: non-regimental, Wilson's tartan list 1819, 23; origin of regimental tartan, 29, 166, 169; chart of sett, 78
Gordon Highlanders, 163
Gow (MacGowan) tartan; chart of sett, 78
Graham of Menteith: chart of sett, 79
Graham of Montrose: chart of sett, 79
Grant tartan: 18th century portraits by Richard Waitt, 16; none-specific tartan 16, 18; New Bruce (Wilson's tartan list 1819), 23; chart of sett, 79; woven by the 'Weavers of Kilbarchan', 51; district tartan, 172, 178
Grant of Monymusk tartan, chart of sett, 79
Grant, hunting tartan: chart of sett, 79
Grey, Sandy, a 'Weaver of Kilbarchan,' 51
Gunn tartan, chart of sett, 79; 178
Hamilton tartan: chart of sett, 49, 82
Hamilton hunting tartan: chart of sett, 82
handweaving, weaving a tartan cloth today, 46
hard tartans; 30, 34, 36
Hay & Leith tartan; chart of sett, 82
Heere, Lucas de, description of illustration of Scotsman (1577), 14
Henderson or Mackendrick: chart of sett, 82
Hepburn tartan: chart of sett, 82
Highlanders; 13, 14, 15-16, 20, 22
Highland Light Infantry, 166
Highlands, The; geography, 10; de-population, 23
Highland Games, 184
Hogarth of Firhill tartan, 178
Home tartan: chart of sett, 82
Hope Vere tartan; chart of sett, 82
Hunt tartan; Wilson's tartan list 1819, 23
Hunter tartan: chart of sett, 82
hunting tartans; evolution, 45
Huntley tartan; chart of sett, 83; 172
indigo — see: dyes, blue
Ingles, Inglis tartan: chart of sett, 83
Innes, MacInnes; chart of sett, 83; hunting tartan, 178
Inverary tartan, 172
Inverness tartan: chart of sett, 83; worn by royalty, 163, 173
Irvine tartan: chart of sett, 83
Irish, The: links with Scotland, 10; wars, 11; evidence of Highland dress, 13, 14; former Disarming Act, 20
Jacobite Uprising (1745); 10, 16, 18, 20, 158
James II, 18
James III; tartan material supplied for his use, 158
James IV: annexed title MacDonald, Lord of the Isles to crown, 158
James V: list of materials for his Highland dress, 13
Jardine tartan, 178
Johnson, Dr. Samuel: description of Highland Dress (1783), 23
Johnstone, Johnston tartan: chart of sett, 83
Johore tartan, 174, 176
Keith & Austin tartan: chart of sett, 83

Kennedy tartan: chart of sett, 86
Kerr, Carr tartan: chart of sett, 86
Kidd, Kid, Kydd tartan: chart of sett, 86
Kilgour tartan: chart of sett, 86
Kilt; 13, 14, 23, 26, 30, 34, 50, 53, 170, 171
Kincaid tartan: chart of sett, 87; 178
Kings Own Scottish Borderers, 163
Kyrtle (tunic), 12
Lamond, Lamont tartan: chart of sett, 87
lanolin (natural grease in wool: removal before dyeing), 41
Largs tartan, 172
Lasting tartan; Wilson's tartan list 1819, 23
Lauder tartan: chart of sett, 87
Lauder, Thomas Dick: 'Lauder Transcript', 24, 25
Leask tartan, 178
leine croich (shirt), 10
Leith tartan (see Hay & Leith), 172
Lennox tartan: chart of sett, 87; 173
Lenzie tartan, 172
Leslie tartan: chart of sett, 90; worn by Scots regiment, 163
Leslie hunting tartan: chart of sett, 90
lichens: use of lichens in dyeing, 42
Lindsay tartan: chart of sett, 90
Livingstone, Livingstone tartan: chart of sett, 90
Lochaber tartan; Wilson's tartan list 1819, 23
Loch Laggan tartan, 172
Logan, James: tartan researcher, 24
Logan &/or **MacLennan** tartan; chart of sett, 91
Wilson's tartan list 1819, 23
London Highland Society: 22; acquirement of tartan samples, 24
looms: used by 'The Weavers of Kilbarchan', 50, 51
Lord Lyon; meeting with James Logan, 24; control of tartans; 29; stipulating only two royal tartans, 158; recording Canadian tartans, 174, 178; his duties, 178; inauguration of The Scottish Tartans Society, 182
Lowlands, The; 13, 14, 28
Lowlanders; 14, 23, 170-71
Lumsden tartan: chart of sett, 91
Mac...: addition of 'Mac' to surname, 52
MacAlister tartan: 'bleeding' of colours; 45; chart of sett, 91
MacAlpine, King Kenneth: beginning of Scottish Kingdom, 11
MacAlpine tartan: chart of sett, 94
MacArthur tartan: chart of sett, 94
MacAuly tartan: chart of sett, 94
MacAulay hunting tartan: chart of sett, 94
MacBean, MacBain tartan: chart of sett, 95; 178
MacBeth tartan: sett, 49; chart of sett, 95; royal connections, 163
Maccallum, Maccullum (also Malcolm) tartan: chart of sett, 95
Maccoll tartan: chart of sett, 95
MacDermot, Macdiarmid: chart of sett, 95
MacDonald clan tartan: chart of sett, 98; 172
MacDonald of Ardnamurchan: chart of sett, 98
MacDonald of Boisdale: chart of sett, 98
MacDonald of Clanranald: chart of sett, 98; 178
MacDonald of Glenaladale: chart of sett, 98
MacDonald of Glengarry: chart of sett, 99
MacDonald of Keppoch: sett, 49; chart of sett, 99; links with Prince Charles Edward, 163
MacDonald of Kingsburgh: chart of sett, 99; links with Prince Charles Edward, 163
MacDonald, Lord of the Isles: 29; chart of sett, 99; Prince Charles' tartan, 158, 163
MacDonald, Lord of the Isles, hunting tartan: chart of sett, 99
MacDonald of Sleat tartan: chart of sett, 99
MacDonnel, Alasdair Ruadh: The Young Glengarry, 26
MacDonnel, Iain, Chief of Glengarry 1720, 26
MacDougal tartan: chart of sett, 102
MacDuff tartan: chart of sett, 102; royal connections, 163
MacDuff dress tartan: chart of sett, 102
Macewen, Macewan tartan: chart of sett, 103
MacFarlane tartan: chart of sett, 103; 178
Macfie, Macphee tartan: chart of sett, 103
MacGillivray tartan: chart of sett, 103; 172
MacGregor tartan: chart of sett, 106
MacGregor Rob Roy tartan: small repeat in sett; 33; many repeats across warp, 46; explanation of sett, 49, 53; chart of sett, 106
MacGregor hunting tartan: chart of sett, 106
MacHardy tartan: chart of sett, 106
MacInnes tartan: chart of sett, 106; 178
MacIntyre tartan: 178
Maciver tartan: chart of sett, 107
Mackay tartan: chart of sett, 107
Mackeane, Maciain tartan: chart of sett, 110
Mackellar tartan: chart of sett, 110
Mackenzie tartan: chart of sett, 110; woven in Kilbarchan, 51; 178
MacKerrell of Hill House hunting tartans: 178
Mackinlay tartan: chart of sett, 110
Mackinnon tartan: chart of sett, 110; 178
Mackintosh clan tartan: chart of sett, 111; 172
Mackintosh, The (Chief): chart of sett, 111
Mackintosh hunting tartan: chart of sett, 111
MacIntyre & Glenorchy: chart of sett, 111
Maclachlan tartan: chart of sett, 114
Maclaine of Lochbuie: chart of sett, 114
MacLaren tartan: chart of sett, 115; royal connections, 163
MacLean tartan, 172

MacLean of Duart: woven in Kilbarchan, 51; chart of sett, 115
MacLeod tartan: chart of sett, 118; 172
MacLeod, Malcolm: waistcoat fragment of Prince Charles Edward's, 20
MacLintock tartan: chart of sett, 118
MacMillan tartan: sett, 49; chart of sett, 118
MacNab tartan: chart of sett, 119
MacNaughton tartan: chart of sett, 119
MacNeil tartan: chart of sett, 122; 172
MacNeil of Barra tartan: chart of sett, 122
MacNeil of Colonsay tartan: chart of sett, 122
MacNicol, Nicholson tartan: chart of sett, 122
Macorqudale tartan: chart of sett, 122
MacPhail tartan: chart of sett, 123
Macpherson, Andrew, 19th Chief of Clan Chattan: description of portrait, 18
Macpherson tartan: Caledonian tartan, Wilson's list 1819, 23; chart of sett, 123
MacQuarrie tartan: sett, 49; chart of sett, 123
MacQueen tartan: chart of sett, 123
MacRae tartan; chart of sett, 126
MacTaggart tartan: chart of sett, 126
MacTavish tartan: chart of sett, 126
MacThomas tartan: chart of sett, 126; 178
Maitland tartan: chart of sett, 127; royal connections, 163; 178
Malcolm tartan: chart of sett, 127
Maple Leaf tartan, 176
Mar tribe tartan: chart of sett, 127; 173; 178
Martin, Martin: extract from 'Western Isles of Scotland' (1703), 15
Matheson tartan: chart of sett, 130
Maxwell tartan: chart of sett, 130
Meikle, William: a 'Weaver of Kilbarchan', 51
Melville tartan: chart of sett, 130
Menzies tartan: sett 49; chart of sett, 130
Middleton tartan: chart of sett, 130
Military References: early dress, 13, 14, 16, 164-166; uniform, 158; tartans for different Scottish Highland regiments, 163, 165-170; Lowland regimental dress, 170, 171; Highland dress in recent military service, 171; overseas tartans derived from Scottish soldiers, 174; The Seige of Secundrabagh, 183
Mitchell tartan: 131
Modern tartans: explanation, 52
Moffat tartan: chart of sett, 131; 172
Moncreiffe tartan: sett, 49: chart of sett, 131; 178
Montgomery, Montgomerie tartan: chart of sett, 131
mordants: derivation of name, use in dyeing and origin, 41
Morgan tartan: chart of sett, 131
Morrison tartan: chart of sett, 134; 178
Mowat, Mowatt tartan: chart of sett, 134
muckle-wheel; 38, 39
Muir tartan: chart of sett, 134
Mull tartan, 172
Munro tartan: woven by 'The Weavers of Kilbarchan' 51; chart of sett, 134
Murray tartan: woven by Wilson's of Bannockburn, 23
Murray of Athol tartan: chart of sett, 135
Murray of Elibank tartan: chart of sett, 135
Murray of Tullibardine tartan: chart of sett, 135
Musselburgh tartan, 172
Nairn tartan, 173
Napier tartan: chart of sett, 135
Nesbitt, Nisbet tartan: chart of sett, 138
Nithsdale tartan: chart of sett, 138; 172
non-specific tartans, 18
North West Territory tartan, 177
Nova Scotia tartan, 176
Ogilvie of Airlie tartan: size of repeat sett, 33; warping, 46; woven by 'The Weavers of Kilbarchan' 51; chart of sett, 138-139
old colours — see ancient colours
Oliphant tartan: chart of sett, 139
Olympic tartan, 174
Paisley tartan, 172
Perth tartan: Wilson's tartan list 1819, 23; district tartan, 172
photographs: explanation, 52
Picts: 11, 16
pivot points: explanation, 53
plaid, the; 10, 13, 14, 15, 16, 18, 26, 30, 164, 165, 166
plain weave; 30, 31
Proscription; 18, 20, 22-23, 26, 158, 166
Ramsay tartan: chart of sett, 139
Ramsay hunting tartan: chart of sett, 139
rank: denoted by tartans, 10,58
Rattray tartan: chart of sett, 139; 178
Rawlinson, Thomas: development of the kilt, 26
'Recuil de la diversité des habits' (1562): record of Highland wear, 14
'Redshanks': description of Highlander and Irish, 14
Renwick tartan, 173
Ritch tartan: Wilson's tartan list 1819, 23
Robertson tartan: chart of sett, 142; 172
roll (rolag): mass of fibre for handspinning, 36
Rollo tartan: chart of sett, 142
Romanes & Patterson, Edinburgh merchants: list of stock (1831), 34
Rose dress tartan: chart of sett, 142; 178
Rose hunting tartan: chart of sett, 143
Ross tartan: woven by Wilson's of Bannockburn, 23; chart of sett, 143
Rothesay, Duke of: 29; Prince Charles' tartan, 158, 163, 173
Royal links with tartans: special usage, 10; Queen Victoria, 29; Royal tartans, 158, 163, 171, 173

Royal Scots; 163, 164
Royal Stewart tartan: sett, 49; English Royal connections, 158
Roxburgh tartan, 172
Russell tartan; 143
Ruthven tartan: chart of sett, 143
Sacheverell, William, Governor of Isle of Man: description of Scottish Highlander (1689), 15
'Saga of Magnus Barefoot' (AD 1093): references to early Highland dress, 11
saxony wheel: see flyer wheel
scale of sett, 33
'Scotia Antiqua' (1643 by Blaeu: descriptions of Highland dress), 16
Scots Guards; 163; 171
Scott tartan: chart of sett, 146
Scott, Sir Walter; 10, 18, 25, 28
'Scottish Gael, The', (1831 by James Logan), 24
Scottish Tartans Society; 23, 29, 182, 183
Scrymgeour tartan: chart of sett, 146
Seaforth Highlanders, 166
selvedges, 47
sept: dependent clan family, 10
Seton tartan: chart of sett, 146
setts: explanation, 33; used by 'The Weavers of Kilbarchan', 50; variations in photographs, 52; 'reading' the setts, 53; sett charts, 54-155
Shaw tartan: chart of sett, 146
Shaw of Tordarroch tartan: chart of sett, 147; 178
sheep: wool from different breeds, 34
shepherd's tartans, 28
Sinclair tartan: chart of sett, 147; 178
Skene tartan: chart of sett, 147
Smith tartan: chart of sett, 147
Sobieski Brothers, 24-25
soft tartans, 34
Somerville tartan: chart of sett, 147
special tartans: worn by clan chiefs, 13
Speed, John, (1552-1629): description of map, 16
spinning, 35-39; spinning wheels, 38
sporran; 12, 26, 170
St. Andrews tartan: Royal connections, 163, 173
Stewart of Appin tartan: chart of sett, 150
Stewart of Athol tartan: chart of sett, 150
Stewart, black tartan, 150
Stuart of Bute tartan, sett, 49; chart of sett, 150
Stewart, dress (Victoria) tartan: sett, 49; chart of sett, 150;
Stewart, Fingask tartan: chart of sett, 150
Stuart of Galloway tartan: chart of sett, 151; worn by Scots regiment, 163
Stewart, old or ancient: chart of sett, 151
Stuart, Royal: chart of sett, 151 (see also Royal Stewart)
Stewart, Donald: quote from 'Scotland's Forged Tartans', 26
Stewart, D.W.; comment in 'Family Portraits' on non-specific tartans, 18
Stirling and Bannockburn, 173
Strathclyde tartan, 172
Strathearn tartan: chart of sett, 154; Royal connections, 163, 173
Strathspey tartan, 173
Sutherland tartan: chart of sett, 154; 173
tartaine: original name for tartan, 10
Taylor tartan: chart of sett, 154
Taylor, John: description of Highland dress (1618), 15
Thomson tartan; 154, 178
Thorburn, W.A.; extract from 'Military Origins of Scottish National Dress', 165
thread count, 53
Tielssch, Hieronymous: travel album's description of Highland Chief, 16
trews (tartan trousers): 10-11, 13, 14, 16, 18, 26, 170, 171
Tweedside tartan, 172
twist: fibres for spinning, 39; use of flyer spinning wheel for twisting, 39
Urquhart tartan: chart of sett, 154
USA Bi-Centennial tartan, 177
Vestiarium Scoticum, 25, 26, 52
Victoria, Queen and Prince Albrt; 29, 158, 170, 182
Waggrall tartan: Wilson's tartan list, 1819, 23; chart of sett, 155
Waitt, Richard: portrait painter, 16
Wallace tartan: chart of sett, 155
warping, 46
Watson tartan, chart of sett, 155
weavers: influence in colour and design of tartan, 15; keeping up with demand for tartans, 23; patterns taken from 'Vestiarium Scoticum', 25; records of early tartans, 52
'Weavers of Kilbarchan, The': from 'In Scotland Again' by H.V. Morton (1933), 50
Wellington tartan: chart of sett, 155
Wemyss tartan: chart of sett, 155
whorl, 38
Wilkie, Sir David: reference to portrait of George IV, 23
Wilson tartan: chart of sett, 155
Wilson's of Bannockburn (commercial weavers) (1720-1976); 23, 52, 172
Wolfe, Major James, 18
Wool: source of, 34; for use in Highland knitting and soft tartans; 36; preparation for dyeing, 41
worsted cloth; 34, 35, 36
Wright, Michael: description of portrait (circa 1660) of Highland Chief, 16